Increasing Access to Rural Finance in Bangladesh

Increasing Access to Rural Finance in Bangladesh

The Forgotten "Missing Middle"

THE WORLD BANK
Washington, D.C.

1818 H Street NW
Washington DC 20433
Telephone: 202-473-1000
Internet: www.worldbank.org
E-mail: feedback@worldbank.org

ISBN: 978-0-8213-7333-0
eISBN: 978-0-8213-7334-7
DOI: 10.1596/978-0-8213-7333-0

Cover photos: S. M. A. Hye Shapan, *Daily Menabzamin* and *Andrew Biraj*.
Cover design: Quantum Think.

Library of Congress Cataloging-in-Publication Data

Ferrari, Aurora.
 Increasing access to rural finance in Bangladesh : the forgotten "missing middle"/by Aurora Ferrari.
  p. cm.
 Includes bibliographical references and index.
 ISBN 978-0-8213-7333-0—ISBN 978-0-8213-7334-7 (electronic)
 1. Rural credit—Bangladesh. 2. Agricultural credit—Bangladesh. 3. Banks and banking—Bangladesh. 4. Financial institutions—Bangladesh. 5. Rural industries—Bangladesh. I. Title.
 HG187.B3F37 2007
 332.7'1095492—dc22   2007039297

Contents

Boxes

Figures

Tables

Acknowledgments

This report was prepared by a World Bank team led by Aurora Ferrari under the overall guidance of Simon Bell, Sadiq Ahmed, Christine Wallich, and Xian Zhu. Major contributors to the report were Shamsuddin Ahmad, Mukta Joshi, Sadruddin Muhammad Salman, and Andrew Lovegrove. In addition the team was composed of Richard Meyer, Olivier Mahul, Mehanz Safavian, Willian Dick, Henry Bagazonzya, Gabi George Afram, Guillemette Sidonie Jaffrin, Shah Nur Quayyum, Sukhinder Arora, and Shahnila Azher. Administrative support was provided by Maria Marjorie Espiritu and Bridget Rosario. The report was funded by the U.K. Department for International Development and the World Bank. The report was edited by Paul Holtz.

The report draws on a Rural Micro, Small, and Medium-size Enterprises (MSMEs) Finance Survey undertaken jointly by the World Bank and Business and Finance Consulting (BFC) in association with HB Consultants. It also draws on the following background papers: a) "Delivering Finance to MSMEs in Bangladesh," August 2006, by Michael Kortenbusch from BFC; b) "Microfinance Products for Small and Medium Farmers and Micro and Small Enterprises: Challenges and Opportunities for MFIs in Bangladesh," April 2007, by Dewan Alamgir and Richard Meyer, which is based on six MFI case studies conducted by the authors; and c) "Bangladesh Crop Index-Based Insurance: A Feasibility Study," July 2006, by William Dick, Ornsaran Pomme Manuamorn, and SARMAP.

The peer reviewers were Renate Kloeppinger-Todd, Nathan M. Belete, and Akbar Ali Khan.

The report incorporates extensive suggestions and comments from representatives of the government of Bangladesh, Palli Karma Sahayyak Foundation (PKSF) staff and its participating organizations, and Bangladeshi financial institutions who attended workshops in Dhaka in September 2006, April 2007, and July 2007, at which the findings of the report were presented and discussed.

Abberviations and Acronyms

ASA	a prominent Bangladeshi microfinance institution; the word means "hope"
BASIC	Bank of Small Industries and Commerce
BEES	Bangladesh Extension Education Services
BFC	Business and Finance Consulting
BKB	Bangladesh Krishi Bank
BRAC	Bangladesh Rural Advancement Committee
BRDB	Bangladesh Rural Development Board
BSB	Bangladesh Shilpa Bank
BSBL	Bangladesh Samabaya Bank Limited
BSRS	Bangladesh Shilpa Rin Sangtha
CARB	Center for Action Research–Barind
GDP	gross domestic product
ICICI	India's largest private commercial bank (formerly Industrial Credit and Investment Corporation of India)
MELA	Micro Enterprise Lending and Assistance
MFI	microfinance institution
MSME	micro, small, and medium-size enterprise
MSMF	marginal, small, and medium-size farmer
PKSF	Palli Karma Sahayyak Foundation

PMUK   Padakhep Manobik Unnayan Kendra (Padakhep Center for Human Development)
RAKUB   Rajshahi Krishi Unnayan Bank
SBC   Sadharan Bima Corporation
SBL   Small Business Loan
SEL   Small Enterprise Loan
SOJAG   Samaj O Jathi Gathan
SREESTI   Sustainable Refinancing for Enterprises and Technology Improvement (product of PMUK)

Currency Equivalents

US$1 = 69 taka (as of June 17, 2007)

Executive Summary

Three-quarters of Bangladesh's people live in rural areas, and more than 40 percent of this population lives below the poverty line—making the rural sector central to the country's development. Micro, small, and medium-size enterprises (MSMEs) and marginal, small, and medium-size farmers (MSMFs)—together referred to in this report as the "missing middle"—are the engines of growth in rural Bangladesh, in terms of both current employment and contributions to gross domestic product (GDP) and possible prospects for future development.

In 2004 nonagricultural activities employed 40 percent of rural workers and accounted for more than 50 percent of rural households' income (World Bank 2004). Most of these activities are conducted by MSMEs. Such enterprises help diversify rural incomes by reducing households' vulnerability to weather and seasonality in agriculture. With limited opportunities for creating employment in agriculture, and if an appropriate enabling environment is developed, these enterprises could continue to grow and will lead Bangladesh's rural economy.

Though becoming less important, farming still plays a major role in the rural economy. The sector employs 54 percent of rural workers (Bangladesh Bureau of Statistics 2000a) and accounts for nearly 21 percent of national GDP.[1] Crops account for the lion's share (57 percent) of agricultural GDP.

Table 1. Rural Farming Households and Landholdings

Classification	Land owned (acres)	Rural households		Share of operated land area (percent)
		Number (millions)	Share (percent)	
Landless	<0.05	6.40	33.8	0.0
Landless	0.05–0.49	3.56	18.8	4.5
Marginal	0.5–0.99	2.58	13.7	8.5
Marginal	1.0–1.49	1.86	9.9	10.3
Small	1.5–2.49	1.99	10.5	17.9
Medium	2.5–7.49	2.20	11.6	41.5
Large	7.5+	0.32	1.7	17.3

Source: Agricultural Census of Bangladesh 1996/97.

About 45 percent of Bangladeshi farmers own between 0.5 and 7.5 acres of land—making them marginal, small, or medium-size (table 1). More than half of farmers own less than 0.5 acre of land and are considered landless. With their extremely limited landholdings and highly volatile incomes, such farmers can make only a limited contribution to rural growth. Indeed, future agricultural growth will depend on intensifying current practices, expanding irrigated areas, and diversifying into higher-value crops—all of which require landholdings larger than 0.5 acre.

Access to Finance: A Major Constraint on Rural Growth

Considerable investment is needed for Bangladesh's agriculture sector to become more commercial and for its nonagricultural activities to grow. MSMEs and MSMFs not only need access to finance for investment, they also need it in a timely fashion to take advantage of market and investment opportunities. And given the high weather risk inherent in agricultural investments, financial institutions need to be able to transfer part of that risk to profitably lend to the segment.

Yet 53 percent of rural enterprises (both agricultural and nonagricultural) consider access to finance a major or very severe obstacle to their operations (World Bank 2003). Making matters worse, no agricultural insurance scheme exists in Bangladesh. About two-thirds of the financing (working capital and new investment) needs of both small and medium-size enterprises are met through internal funds or retained earnings (figure 1). Thus most enterprises rely on household and business savings to expand—even for working capital. Although this might be the best solution in the current environment, there are limits to equity-financed growth.

Box 1

How Do Natural Disasters Affect Rice Production?

Flooding is a recurrent event in Bangladesh. Most of its territory consists of floodplains, and up to 30 percent of the country experiences annual flooding during the monsoon season—while periodic extreme floods affect 60 percent of the national territory. Although annual flooding is beneficial, severe flooding hurts the population and causes major losses in rice production.

Rice crops have, however, become less susceptible to flood damage as the area planted with deepwater aman rice (grown on flood-prone land during the monsoon season) has fallen and boro rice (which can be produced five to six months after a flood-damaged rice harvest) has been planted more extensively. Production losses caused by floods mainly affect aus and aman (rainfed) rice, while losses for boro rice are limited to unusual events. For example, the 2000 flood caused an estimated loss of 305,482 metric tons of aman and only 7,920 metric tons of boro. Losses caused by cyclones follow the opposite pattern, with boro rice most affected. For example, it is estimated that cyclones in 2000 caused a loss of 318,460 metric tons of boro and no damage to aus and aman crops.

Bangladesh is also vulnerable to recurrent droughts. Some 2.3 million hectares are prone to drought, and between 1960 and 1991 droughts occurred 19 times. Two critical dry periods are distinguished:

- Rabi and pre-Karif drought (between January and May), due to the cumulative effects of dry days, higher temperatures during pre-Karif, and low availability of soil moisture.
- Karif droughts (between June/July and October), created by sub-humid and dry conditions in the country's highlands and medium highlands. Rainfall shortages affect the critical reproductive stages of the transplanted aman crop in December, reducing its yield—particularly in areas with where soil has low moisture-holding capacity.

Western regions are especially vulnerable to droughts. During the Rabi season 1.2 million hectares of cropland face droughts of various magnitudes, and a severe drought can damage more than 40 percent of broadcast aus. During the Kharif season drought causes significant damage to the transplanted aman crop on about 2.3 million hectares. In addition to causing agricultural losses, droughts significantly increase land degradation.

Source: Bureau of Statistics data.

Figure 1. Most Rural Enterprises Rely on Internal Sources for Financing

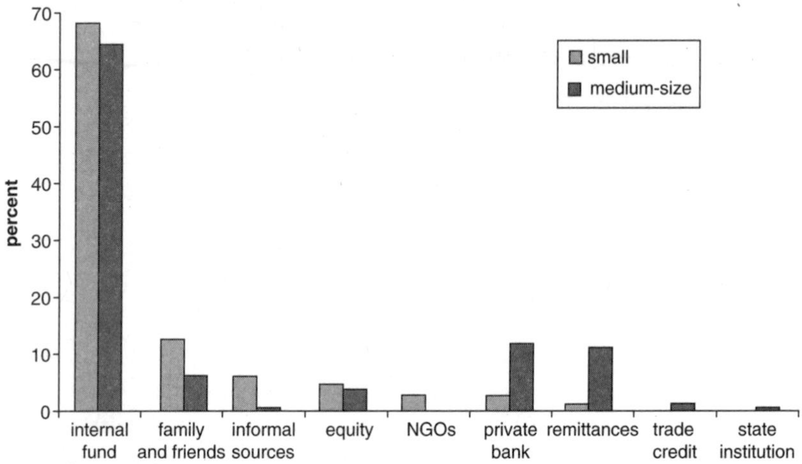

Source: World Bank 2003.

Increasing access to rural finance is often the last frontier for financial sector development in developing countries. Financial institutions aiming to operate in rural areas in these countries usually have to deal with high transaction costs, low population densities, remote areas, and a heavy focus on agriculture, with related weather and commodity risks (box 1). Although Bangladesh is highly vulnerable to natural disasters—including floods, droughts, and cyclones—its high population density lowers transaction costs considerably (though not entirely).

This report seeks to:

- Measure the quantity and quality of access to finance by rural MSMEs and MSMFs. In Bangladesh these are also referred to as the "missing middle"—a segment not served by banks or microfinance institutions (MFIs).
- Identify constraints that financial institutions face in serving MSMEs and MSMFs. The institutions analyzed in detail include, Bangladesh Krishi Bank (BKB), Rajshahi Krishi Unnayan Bank (RAKUB), MFIs, private banks, and insurance companies. These institutions have been selected because they are among the largest providers of finance to the missing middle. Moreover, given their size, they have a considerable impact on the current dysfunction of rural financial markets.
- Develop a realistic strategy and options for sustainably increasing access to finance for the missing middle.

Lending to the Missing Middle: Supply-Side Evidence

Bangladesh's banking sector has grown quickly since 1995, with bank assets growing by nearly 23 percent a year between 1995 and 2005. Moreover, the banking sector grew faster than GDP during this period, with loans rising from 21 to 30 percent of GDP and deposits jumping from 26 to 39 percent of GDP. Yet this expansion has not really benefited the missing middle.

Over the years the government has introduced several initiatives aimed at facilitating rural credit in general, and lending to the missing middle in particular. These include:

- Creating BKB in 1973 and RAKUB in 1987 to serve rural areas and the Bank of Small Industries and Commerce (BASIC) in 1988 to promote small-scale industries in rural and urban areas.
- Promoting two systems of cooperatives since 1972.
- Providing refinance facilities to institutions interested in financing agriculture.
- Introducing a policy encouraging banks—especially private ones—to expand their branches and activities in rural areas.
- Creating a multiperil crop insurance scheme and waiving principal and interest on small agricultural loans from state banks and cooperatives in case of natural disasters.

But government efforts to increase access to finance have had mixed results. The importance of banks and cooperatives in rural lending has declined, while the importance of MFIs has increased. Bank intermediation in rural areas remains limited, with banks transferring 0.5 taka to urban areas for each 1 taka in deposits collected in rural areas. The largest providers of agricultural loans, BKB and RAKUB, are deeply insolvent, and BASIC and the cooperative system are irrelevant in terms of rural loans. Finally, since the closure of the government-sponsored crop insurance scheme, insurance companies have been almost completely absent from rural markets.

No data are available on bank lending to MSMEs and MSMFs, but evidence indicates that such lending is limited. Moreover, the microfinance sector—traditionally the largest provider of small loans in rural areas—has remained focused on the landless poor with group loans involving weekly repayments. Such products are not suitable for MSMEs and MSMFs.

Lending to the Missing Middle: Demand-Side Evidence

A 2006 survey of rural MSMEs found that despite substantial use of bank services among these enterprises (43 percent had an account, and

75 percent made transfers), during 2003–06 only 32 percent borrowed from banks. During the same period 16 percent of these enterprises borrowed from MFIs and 8 percent from informal sources (mainly family and friends)—while 44 percent did not borrow at all. When borrowing from banks, the average loan for such enterprises is 400,000 taka, while their average loan from MFIs is 38,000 taka.

These firms financed 88 percent of their working capital needs using retained earnings and internal funds, and only 33 percent used debt to finance new investments. Thus, instead of borrowing, most MSMEs expand their activities only after building up internal resources.

Micro, small, and medium-size enterprises do not seem to be excluded from financial markets because of poor financial performance. Indeed, such enterprises have strong returns on capital and robust long-term profitability. Instead, they seem to be excluded due to a gap in the financial market.

When asked why they did not apply for credit, 40 percent of these enterprises cited the high costs, direct and indirect. Direct costs include interest rates and other transaction costs (such as for documentation, including financial statements, titles, and the like). Indirect costs include long processing times (which translate into missed business opportunities) and intensive application processes requiring many meetings between borrowers and banks (again translating into missed opportunities). Once all the required documents have been submitted, it takes an average of 40 days to get a loan from a bank and 28 days from an MFI. In addition, the survey found that banks mainly require immovable assets as primary collateral in 86 percent of cases, while movable assets account for 73 percent of the average asset value of MSMEs.

Similarly, a 2002 agricultural credit survey found that 34–40 percent of medium-size farmers (depending on their acreage) have no access to credit. The survey showed that larger farmers tend to borrow from formal and informal sources more than small farmers do. About 22 percent of landless farmers had formal or informal loans, compared with 38 percent of large farmers.

Not surprisingly, access to bank credit increases with farm size, while access to microcredit decreases. But the average loan per acre declines with increasing farm acreage. In line with this, farmers that use both bank and informal loans borrow less from banks than from informal sources. As with MSMEs, the total cost of borrowing for MSMFs is much higher, on average, than is advertised by banks. Advertised annual interest rates range from 8 to 12 percent, while the total cost of borrowing (including transport, documentation, and bribes) is closer to 25 percent.

Why Have Government Efforts to Increase Access to Finance Failed for the Missing Middle?

BKB and RAKUB, which are supposed to be the main providers of financial services in rural areas, are deeply insolvent. A government refinance facility that should have facilitated agricultural lending has instead become the main source of funding for BKB and RAKUB's growing capital deficits, and agricultural lending is falling—compromising their capacity to serve the missing middle.

Private banks have high enough earnings from corporate lending that they have limited appetite to expand into rural areas. Although required to open one rural branch for every four in urban areas, private banks use rural branches to collect deposits that are then used for loans in urban areas. Most lending opportunities in rural areas involve MSMEs and MSMFs, which banks cannot serve profitably under the current legal and regulatory framework and with current lending methodologies. Although lending profitably to these enterprises is not easy, doing so for such farmers is even more challenging because of the difficulties that agricultural lending presents—including weather risks. But such markets are harder to serve profitably with traditional approaches to agricultural insurance due to the lack of financial capacity among rural households, lack of distribution channels, low unit size of transactions, and high operating costs.

Finally, while MFIs operate in rural areas, they focus on the landless and do not have appropriate lending methodologies to serve larger, more complex clients.

How Can the Government Facilitate Increased Access to Finance for the Missing Middle?

A number of policies could increase access to finance for the missing middle. This report offers suggestions that are considered the most pragmatic in the current environment, that have been proven in similar circumstances in other countries, and that could lead to tangible improvements for the missing middle.

Given the historical significance of BKB and RAKUB, any solution to increasing services in rural areas—especially for MSMFs—will necessarily involve these institutions. Their current market-distorting behavior only reinforces the importance of tackling their underlying problems.

In addition to reforming the publicly sponsored financial sector, other useful steps could be taken to facilitate the participation of private financial institutions and MFIs in increasing access to financial services for the missing middle. If the right enabling environment were created with appropriate lending methodologies, private banks could become the main lenders to MSMEs—especially for the top end of the market. But given the current stage of development of the rural banking market, it seems unlikely that private banks will lend to MSMFs in the near future.

With suitable products and technology, MFIs could scale up their lending to MSMEs and MSMFs—especially micro and small enterprises and marginal and small farmers. Indeed, such institutions are likely to focus on the bottom end of these market segments, at least in the medium term.

Finally, with the right enabling environment and development of the right products, the insurance sector could absorb some commercial agricultural risk. In addition, uninsurable financial risk could be covered by the government in a disciplined fashion.

To help banks increase lending to MSMEs, the government could:

- Reform the enabling environment for MSME lending by reviewing rules on provisioning requirements, reforming and implementing a new legal framework for secured transactions, and strengthening the credit bureau's operations.
- Create a technical assistance fund to help selected banks with potential to develop appropriate products and procedures for MSMEs.

To help MFIs increase lending to MSMEs and MSMFs, the government could:

- Set up a technical assistance fund to increase lending to the missing middle, by introducing new products and lending technologies and appropriate management information systems.

To help BKB and RAKUB become the main providers of rural financial services, the government could:

- Reform and recapitalize both banks.

To facilitate risk transfer for institutions lending to MSMFs, the government could:

- Remove the legal and regulatory obstacles to the development of index-based weather insurance.

- Promote the creation of a technical assistance unit that helps interested institutions develop new index-based insurance products.
- Create a Fund for Natural Calamities to cover risk that is not commercially viable.

Note

1. The industrial sector accounts for 27 percent and the service sector, 52 percent (World Bank, World Development Indicators database 2006).

CHAPTER 1

The Missing Middle: Supply-Side Evidence

Over the past 10 years, Bangladesh's banking sector has grown considerably, while overall access to financial services has increased moderately. Despite the booming banking sector and government efforts to increase access in rural areas, rural financial markets have shrunk in relative terms. In addition, access to finance by MSMEs and MSMFs—the "missing middle"— remains limited.

The Financial Sector

Over the past decade Bangladesh's financial sector has grown steadily, with the ratio of M2 (broad money) to GDP—which indicates the degree of monetization with respect to the real economy—reaching 38 percent in 2003 (table 1.1).[1] This level is comparable to that in Pakistan (43 percent) but lower than in India (60 percent). Although Bangladesh's ratio is low in absolute terms, the improving trend suggests that there is growing capacity in the financial sector to channel surplus savings into productive investments.

In 2005 banks in Bangladesh provided domestic credit equal to 44 percent of GDP—again, comparable to Pakistan (also 44 percent) but considerably behind India (61 percent). Bangladesh compares favorably with its peers in terms of domestic credit to the private sector, which in 2005 was

Table 1.1. Indicators for Bangladesh's Financial Sector, 2000–05
(percent)

Indicator	2000	2001	2002	2003	2004	2005
Broad money (M2/GDP)	32	35	37	38	—	—
Liquid liabilities (M3/GDP)	36	37	39	40	42	45
Private credit/GDP	23	24	26	27	—	—
Domestic credit provided by banks/GDP	37	39	40	38	41	44
Domestic credit to private sector/GDP	26	27	29	29	30	32
Financial sector assets/GDP	—	—	—	46.5	51.9	55.4
Bank assets/financial sector assets	—	—	—	87.6	90.3	90.4

Source: World Bank, Financial Sector Development Indicators and World Development Indicators database.
Note: — = not available.

32 percent of GDP, versus 28 percent in Pakistan and 41 percent in India. (Similarly, in 2003 private credit as a share of GDP was 27 percent in Bangladesh, 22 percent in Pakistan, and 31 percent in India.) Pakistan's lower share shows that there is more "crowding out" in credit markets by state institutions.

By the end of 2005 financial sector assets were equal to 55 percent of Bangladesh's GDP. Banks account for 90 percent of financial sector assets. Other parts of the financial sector remain largely undeveloped. For example, the market capitalization of equity markets averaged just 4 percent of GDP during 1999–2004. And in the insurance sector, premiums equaled only 0.61 percent of GDP in 2003—the lowest level in Asia. (In India this share was 3.14 percent; in Pakistan it was 0.67 percent.)

For products other than life insurance, the insurance sector is dominated by Sadharan Bima Corporation (SBC), a state-owned insurance corporation with 21 percent market share—and 51 percent market share when reinsurance is included. But the non-life insurance sector is very small (total premiums equaled 0.2 percent of GDP in 2005), highly segmented (with 43 companies, 10 of which account for two-thirds of market share), and has mixed profitability (with the 10 largest companies generating net profits of 12–14 percent of gross premiums in 2005, while the average return for the entire industry was about 6 percent [AXCO 2006]).

Access to insurance is quite limited. In 2005 estimated premium income per capita was $0.8 for non-life and $1.7 for life insurance. By comparison, estimated premium income per capita for non-life and for life insurance were $4.4 and $18.3 in India and $1.8 and $2.9 in Pakistan (Swiss Re 2006).

The Banking Sector

In 2005 Bangladesh had 48 banks, 9 of which were owned by the state.[2] The nine state-owned institutions include four nationalized commercial banks (Agrani Bank, Janata Bank, Rupali Bank, and Sonali Bank) and five development financial institutions, two of which (BKB and RAKUB) were created to meet credit needs in rural areas, two (Bangladesh Shilpa Bank [BSB] and Bangladesh Shilpa Rin Sangtha [BSRS]) to target the industrial sector, and the fifth (BASIC) to meet the needs of small and medium-size enterprises in both urban and rural areas. In 2005 the nationalized commercial banks and development financial institutions accounted for 47 percent of total bank assets, or 812 billion taka, and 48 percent of deposits, or 683 billion taka.[3] In addition, 30 private commercial banks and 9 foreign banks had 915 billion taka in assets and 733 billion taka in deposits.

The banking sector has grown quickly since 1995, with bank assets growing by nearly 23 percent a year between 1995 and 2005—though this slowed to average annual growth of 11 percent between 2000 and 2005 (figure 1.1). The banking sector grew faster than GDP between 1995 and 2005, with loans rising from 21 to 30 percent of GDP and deposits jumping from 26 to 39 percent of GDP (figure 1.2). Bank credit grew by an annual average of 18 percent between 2000 and 2005, outpacing the growth in bank assets during this period by nearly

Figure 1.1. Bank Assets, 1995–2006

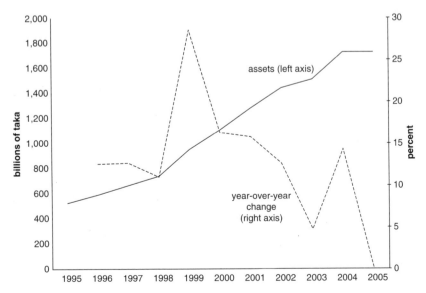

Figure 1.2. Change in Bank Loans and Deposits, 1995–2005

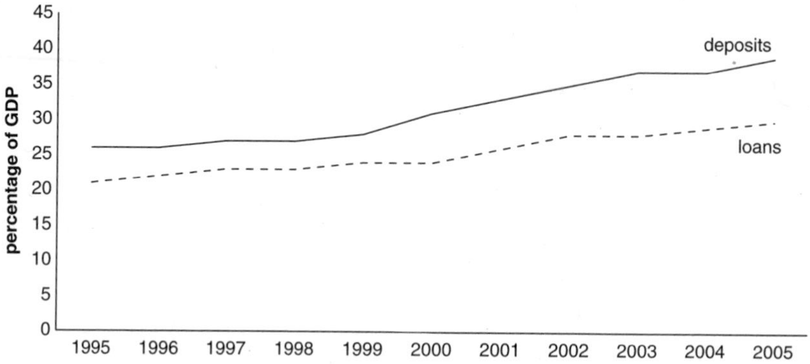

Source: Bangladesh Bank 2006c.

57 percent and indicating that banks have been steadily redeploying funds from non-credit assets into loans.

Despite the rapid growth of banks, indicators of access—such as deposit accounts and loan accounts per 1,000 people—grew only moderately between 2001 and 2005. Deposit accounts increased from 232 to 237 per 1,000 people, while loan accounts rose from 57 to 60 per 1,000 people. In India during this period, deposit accounts per 1,000 people grew from 417 to 432 and loan accounts per 1,000 people from 51 to 71. Moreover, between 1996 and 2005 total deposits as a share of broad money (M2) remained flat, at 86 percent. Ideally, this ratio should increase as more people are exposed to the formal financial sector and decide to open deposit accounts rather than hold cash.

Bangladesh's banking sector is in effect two banking systems: a private one that is reasonably healthy, profitable, and focused on urban markets and a state-owned one that is largely insolvent, unprofitable, and the main provider of banking services in rural areas. Indeed, the four nationalized commercial banks account for 56 percent of rural branches, and the two rural banks (RAKUB and BKB) for 28 percent.

Further analysis highlights the contrast between state and private banks. Since 2000 the capital adequacy ratios of nationalized commercial banks have steadily deteriorated, while private commercial banks and development financial institutions have generally maintained theirs slightly above the minimum of 9 percent (table 1.2). And foreign banks have had high and steadily rising ratios, reaching 26 percent in 2005.

In addition, since 2000 returns on assets and equity have steadily declined for state banks, reaching –0.1 percent and –6.9 percent for

Table 1.2. Capital Adequacy Ratios of Banks, 2000–05

(percent)

	2000	2001	2002	2003	2004	2005
Nationalized commercial banks	4.4	4.2	4.1	4.3	4.1	–4
Development finance institutions	3.2	3.9	6.9	7.7	9.1	9.2
Private commercial banks	10.9	9.9	9.7	10.5	10.3	9.1
Foreign banks	18.4	16.8	21.4	22.9	24.2	26
Average	6.7	6.7	7.5	8.4	8.7	7.3

Source: Bangladesh Bank 2006a.

nationalized commercial banks and –0.1 percent and –2.0 percent for development financial institutions in 2005 (table 1.3). During the same period private banks improved their performance, with private commercial banks increasing their returns on assets and equity to 1.1 percent and 18.1 percent and foreign banks raising theirs to 3.1 percent and 18.4 percent.

The poor and deteriorating condition of state banks is due to:

- Weak governance—for example, boards of directors are political appointees,[4] and periodic announcements of interest and sometimes principal repayment waivers encourage a culture of nonpayment among borrowers (in the expectation of future waivers).[5]
- Weak management, often also politically appointed.
- A wide variety of operating weaknesses, including inadequate or nonexistent information technology, ineffective control systems, and antiquated credit and risk management.

Finally, despite the seemingly better performance of private banks, reported capital adequacy ratios and earnings for both state and private banks do not reflect their real status. The discrepancy between banks' reported data and real performance is caused by three factors. First, classified loans and assets are widely underreported due to weak controls and poor information technology. Second, Bangladesh's accounting standards are much less stringent than international standards. Third, some banks fail to make even the loan loss provisions required by the country's weak regulations.[6]

For the banking sector as a whole, Bangladesh Bank estimates that in 2005 the shortfall in provisions (that is, provisions required by regulation but not made) totaled 45.7 billion taka—just over half of the sector's aggregate capital and reserves. For example, nationalized commercial banks and development financial institutions have reported declining

Table 1.3. Returns on Assets and Equity for Banks, 2000–05

	2000	2001	2002	2003	2004	2005
Return on asssets (percent)						
Nationalized commercial banks	0.1	0.1	0.1	0.1	−0.1	−0.1
Development finance institutions	−3.7	0.7	0.3	0	−0.2	−0.1
Private commercial banks	0.8	1.1	0.8	0.7	1.2	1.1
Foreign banks	2.7	2.8	2.4	2.6	3.2	3.1
Average	0	0.7	0.5	0.5	0.7	0.6
Return on equity (percent)						
Nationalized commercial banks	1.7	2.4	4.2	3.0	−5.3	−6.9
Development finance institutions	−68.0	12.3	5.8	−0.6	−2.1	−2.0
Private commercial banks	17.0	20.9	13.6	11.4	19.5	18.1
Foreign banks	27.3	32.4	21.5	20.4	22.5	18.4
Average	0.3	15.9	11.6	9.8	13.0	12.4

Source: Bangladesh Bank 2006a.

nonperforming loans since 1998 (table 1.4), but these data are inconsistent with their reported returns on assets and equity (see table 1.3). The latter returns strongly suggest that the cash flows of state banks have become increasingly negative, indicating that nonperforming loans are actually increasing.[7]

Government Efforts to Increase Rural Credit

To ensure that the growth of the banking sector is balanced between urban and rural areas and between smaller and larger clients, Bangladesh's government has introduced quite a few initiatives aimed at facilitating rural credit in general, and lending to the missing middle in particular.

Creating banks to serve rural areas

The government created BKB in 1973 and RAKUB in 1987 to serve rural areas, and BASIC in 1988 to promote small industries in urban and rural areas.[8] BKB and RAKUB play a key role in delivering financial services to rural households. As noted, in 2005 they accounted for 28 percent of bank branches in rural areas, as well as 23 percent of outstanding bank rural loans and 8 percent of deposits (by volume). In addition to their focus on supporting agricultural activities, both banks engage in commercial and retail business.

Table 1.4. Nonperforming Loans of Banks, 2000–05

(Percentage of total loans)

	2000	2001	2002	2003	2004	2005
Nationalized commercial banks	38.6	37.0	33.7	29.0	25.3	21.4
Development finance institutions	62.6	61.8	56.1	47.4	42.9	34.9
Private commercial banks	22.0	17.0	16.4	12.4	8.5	5.6
Foreign banks	3.4	3.3	2.6	2.7	1.5	1.3
Average	34.9	31.5	28.0	22.1	17.6	13.6

Source: Bangladesh Bank Annual Report 2005–06
Note: Data are reported net of loan loss provisions.

With 947 branches, BKB covers all of Bangladesh except the Rajshahi division—which is covered by RAKUB, with 357 branches. Both banks are entirely owned by the Ministry of Finance, with state-appointed boards of directors and management.[9] Both banks are also deeply insolvent (see below). With 27 branches across the country, BASIC was created to be the main provider of credit to small industry in urban and rural areas. The bank's bylaws require that half of its loanable funds go to small-scale industries.[10] The bank is the only profitable state-owned bank.

Promoting cooperative networks

The government has promoted two cooperative networks, covering both traditional cooperatives under the Registrar of Cooperatives and financed by Bangladesh Sambaya Bank Limited (BSBL) and two-tier cooperative systems under the Bangladesh Rural Development Board (BRDB).[11] Cooperatives in the two networks are financed through Bangladesh's Bank agricultural refinance facility (for BSBL) and budget allocations (for BRDB).

Cooperatives under BSBL are organized in three tiers: BSBL is the apex cooperative bank, under which there are central cooperative societies and primary societies. BSBL on-lends to the central societies, which in turn on-lend to the primary cooperatives. BRDB, by contrast, organizes cooperative societies into a two-tier structure, with primary cooperatives at the local level and others at the *thana* level. Although allowed, in practice neither cooperative network takes deposits. Rather, both act as credit delivery mechanisms. The Department of Rural Cooperatives and Development oversees the activities of cooperatives.

Providing refinance facilities for agriculture

Through Bangladesh Bank, the government provides refinance facilities to financial institutions interested in financing agriculture. The Agricultural Extension Department sets the terms and conditions for agricultural refinance loans between Bangladesh Bank and participating financial institutions, and between these institutions and farmers (box 1.1). BKB and RAKUB are the only active borrowers from the refinance facility. Although most of the outstanding amount is overdue, Bangladesh Bank continues to extend the facility because BKB and RAKUB's exposure is explicitly guaranteed by the Ministry of Finance. BSBL and BRDB have outstanding (and overdue) loans from the facility but have not been borrowing recently, as they have been unable to repay the amounts outstanding and have no government guarantee for these loans.

Box 1.1

Terms and Conditions of Loans Refinanced under the Agriculture Refinancing Facility

Bangladesh Bank provides a refinance facility for agriculture. At the beginning of each fiscal year, interested banks determine their goals for agricultural lending and submit applications to Bangladesh Bank. The limits for each participating institution are approved by Bangladesh Bank's board of directors, and repayments to the bank are guaranteed by the government. Between 1996 and 2005 annual disbursements from the facility ranged from 6 to 8 billion taka, while cumulative overdue loans increased from 7 billion taka in 2001 to 34 billion taka in 2005. Refinance facilities are offered for three types of loan products:

- Short-term loans (one-year maturities) to cultivate crops (aman, boro, sugarcane, wheat, oil seed, vegetables), jute, maize, cotton, tobacco, fisheries, and the like.
- Medium-term loans (five-year maturities) for livestock and poultry production (dairy, cattle, goat, buffalo, sheep, ducks), fisheries, nurseries, betel leaf cultivation, beef fattening, fruit gardening, and the like.
- Long-term loans (more than five-year maturities) for agricultural equipment, power tillers, deep and shallow tube wells, low lift pumps, hand tube wells, rubber cultivation, and the like.

The final annual interest rate is 8 percent for crop loans, 9 percent for other agricultural loans, and 11.5 percent for medium-size and large agricultural activities. Bangladesh Bank charges the participating financial institutions an annual interest rate of 5 percent.

Encouraging banks to expand activities in rural areas

A recently introduced government policy encourages banks, especially private ones, to expand their activities in rural areas. Bangladesh Bank requires that banks have one rural branch for every four urban ones.

Providing crop insurance and waiving payments on small loans

In the late 1970s the government designed the traditional multiperil crop insurance scheme that was administered by SBC, a state-owned insurance corporation. The program had to be ended in the early 1990s because the scheme was financially unsustainable, with claims 20 times higher than premiums (see chapter 3). Since the program was discontinued, after natural disasters and before elections the government has regularly waived interest, and sometimes principal, on agricultural loans below 5,000 taka disbursed by BKB, RAKUB, BSBL, BRDB, and nationalized commercial banks. In theory the Ministry of Finance should compensate the financial institutions for half of the amount waived; in practice this has almost never happened.

Outcomes of government efforts

Government efforts to increase access to finance have had mixed results. Lending in rural areas has increased, though at a much slower rate than in urban areas. The importance of banks and cooperatives in rural lending has been declining, while the importance of MFIs has increased. Bank intermediation in rural areas remains limited, with banks transferring 0.5 taka to urban areas for every 1.0 taka in deposits collected in rural areas. The largest providers of agricultural loans, BKB and RAKUB, are deeply insolvent; while BASIC, BSBL, and BRDB are irrelevant in terms of rural loan volumes. Finally, since the closure of the government-sponsored crop insurance scheme, insurance companies have been almost totally absent from rural markets. (Appendix 2 presents a comparison of rural lending markets in Bangladesh and India.)

Outstanding loans in rural areas rose 60 percent (by volume) between 2002 and 2005 (the more recent year for which data are available), and rural lending is estimated to account for a third of lending volumes nationwide. During this period MFIs were the fastest-growing financial institutions, with government microfinance programs increasing their loan portfolio by 240 percent and MFIs by 99 percent. Total outstanding bank loans also increased, though by much less—57 percent. Loans from BRDB and BSBL increased by just 5 percent.

In 2005 banks accounted for 74 percent of rural lending volumes, MFIs for 20 percent, BRDB and BSBL for 4 percent, and government microfinance program for 2 percent (figure 1.3). Between 2002 and 2005 the shares in rural lending of banks and of BRDB and BSBL fell, while those of MFIs and government microfinance programs increased.

Within the banking sector, between 2000 and 2005 private banks became more important at the expense of state-owned ones. Still, state-owned banks account for 70 percent of bank loans and 66 percent of bank deposits in rural areas. Sonali Bank is the largest provider of loans and deposit services (by volume) in rural areas. BSB, BSRS, and BASIC account for less than 1 and 0 percent respectively—and their shares have been declining (table 1.5).

Since 1996 growth in rural bank credit has been well below that in urban areas (table 1.6). As a result, rural lending as a share of total bank lending fell from 37 percent in 1996 to 28 percent in 2005 (figure 1.4).

The government's policy of encouraging banks to expand in rural areas has had mixed results. Bank lending has increased in rural areas, yet between 1996 and 2005 the proportion of loans to deposits in rural branches deteriorated sharply as banks increasingly drained deposits from rural areas to finance urban loans (figure 1.5). In 2005, for every taka collected as a deposit by a rural bank branch, only a little over half a taka (0.57) was lent. This proportion was similar for both state (0.6) and private banks (0.5). Moreover, between 1996 and 2005 agricultural loans fell from 17 percent to 10 percent of total bank lending (figure 1.6).

BKB and RAKUB, which were created to be the main providers of financial services in rural areas, are deeply insolvent, as evidenced by growing capital deficits (table 1.7). Given the importance of both banks for rural areas, their insolvency severely undermines the stability of rural financial markets. Both banks' growing capital deficits have been funded by Bangladesh Bank's agriculture refinance facility and 90-day demand

Figure 1.3. Estimated Rural Loans by Source, 2002 and 2005

Source: Authors' estimates based on Bangladesh Bank and PKSF (Palli Karma Sahayyak Foundation) data.

Table 1.5. Bank Lending and Deposits in Rural Areas, 2000 and 2005

Rural Lending, 2000		
Type of bank	Millions of taka	Share of total (percent)
Nationalized commercial banks	109,561	55
BKB, RAKUB	53,353	27
BSB, BSRS, BASIC	1,038	1
Private commercial banks	32,861	17
Foreign banks	668	0
Total	197,481	100

Rural Deposits, 2000		
Type of bank	Millions of taka	Share of total (percent)
Nationalized commercial banks	207,662	68
BKB, RAKUB	26,125	9
BSB, BSRS, BASIC	1,050	0
Private commercial banks	69,132	23
Foreign banks	1,207	0
Total	305,176	100

Rural Lending, 2005		
Type of bank	Millions of taka	Share of total (percent)
Nationalized commercial banks	141,979	46
BKB, RAKUB	72,923	23
BSB, BSRS, BASIC	2,737	1
Private commercial banks	92,079	30
Foreign banks	1,000	0
Total	310,719	100

Rural Deposits, 2005		
Type of bank	Millions of taka	Share of total (percent)
Nationalized commercial banks	317,380	58
BKB, RAKUB	46,432	8
BSB, BSRS, BASIC	2,693	0
Private commercial banks	180,341	33
Foreign banks	2,650	0
Total	549,496	100

Source: Bangladesh Bank data.

Table 1.6. Average Annual Growth in Urban and Rural Bank Loans, 1996–2005

(*percent*)

	1996–2000	2000–05	2004–05
Urban	17.4	20.7	18.4
Rural	10.8	11.5	15.0

Source: Bangladesh Bank, scheduled Statistics April–June 2005.

Figure 1.4. Urban and Rural Shares of Bank Loans, 1996–2005

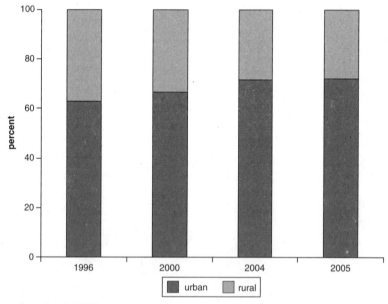

Source: Bangladesh Bank 2006c.

facility.[12] In 2006 BKB and RAKUB's outstanding loans from Bangladesh Bank were equal to its equity.

One of the main causes of BKB and RAKUB's insolvency is an implicit government policy of using the banks as insurers of last resort and as vote banks.[13] As noted, after natural disasters and before elections, interest and sometimes principal on agricultural loans under 5,000 taka are often waived.

Possibly due to waivers of principal and interest and rollovers of overdue loans, the average loan size at BKB and RAKUB fell sharply in real terms between 1996 and 2005 (table 1.8).[14] This fact is also evident from the number of borrower accounts, which is growing more than

Figure 1.5. Proportion of Loans to Deposits by Bank Branch Location, 1996–2005

Source: Bangladesh Bank data.

Figure 1.6. Distribution of Bank Loans by Purpose, 1996–2005

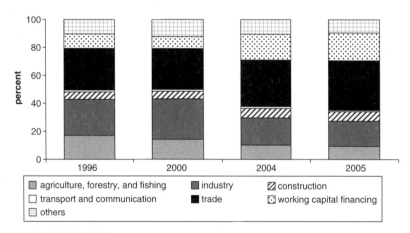

Source: Bangladesh Bank data.

three times faster than the rural population and is partly responsible for the drop in average loan size.

In the 20 years since its creation, BASIC has made no dent in the MSME market segment. During that time the bank has acquired just 2,000 clients, of an estimated 6.8 million MSMEs. Between 2000 and 2005 it added an average of 200 new clients a year, or just over 1 client a month per branch.

Table 1.7. Summary of Audited Financial Statements for BKB and RAKUB, 2005
(millions of taka)

	BKB	RAKUB
Total assets	95,284	30,385
Total loans (private and state sectors)	65,675	21,428
Total deposits	56,344	11,578
Reported capital	−15,519	−98
Total capital shortfall per auditors	−25,989	−2,275
Adjusted capital/total assets (percent)	−16	−7
Borrowings from Bangladesh Bank/total assets (percent)	35	51

Sources: BKB 2005; RAKUB, 2005 audited financial statements.

Table 1.8. Access Indicators for Private Clients of BKB and RAKUB, 1996–2005

	1996	2000	2004	2005	Change, 1996–2005 (percent)
Number of borrower accounts					
BKB	1,724,811	2,647,206	2,872,232	3,050,224	76.8
RAKUB	603,421	725,726	809,862	867,002	43.7
Total	2,328,232	3,372,932	3,682,094	3,917,226	68.2
Outstanding loans in real terms (millions of taka)					
BKB	32,259	40,519	42,038	44,044	36.5
RAKUB	14,322	10,418	13,115	14,592	1.9
Total	46,581	50,937	55,153	58,637	25.9
Average loan size in real terms (taka)					
BKB	18,703	15,307	14,636	14,440	−22.8
RAKUB	23,735	14,355	16,195	16,831	−29.1
Total	20,007	15,101	14,979	14,969	−25.2

Source: BKB and RAKUB data.

The cooperative movement, which was created to increase lending to rural areas, has never really taken off; it accounts for a mere 4 percent of rural lending volumes. In 2006 BSBL was estimated to have just 32 million taka in capital. Moreover, the cooperative movement is almost entirely dependent on external sources—namely, Bangladesh Bank's agricultural refinance facility and, more recently, budget allocations.

Finally, since the end of the government-sponsored crop insurance scheme, insurance companies have almost totally abandoned rural markets.[15] To fill the gap, 60 or so MFIs (including Bangladesh Rural Advancement

Committee [BRAC] and ASA) have developed micro-insurance products, mainly in rural areas, to accompany their lending activities. An estimated 81 micro-insurance plans cover 20 million rural households. But most of these plans are for life and health insurance; only four MFIs offer livestock insurance, and none offers crop insurance. Micro-insurance schemes are self-managed by the institutions and funded by premiums from participating members. The premiums are usually invested in revolving loan funds, with a limited portion invested in banks' fixed term deposits. Premiums are based on specific assumptions, not actuarial calculations.

Lending to the Missing Middle

No data are available on bank lending to the missing middle. But evidence indicates that such lending is limited. First, agricultural lending has been declining for many years. Second, BKB and RAKUB—the largest providers of agricultural loans—have progressively reduced their average loan sizes in real terms to 15,000 taka. Finally, it is estimated

Table 1.9. Microfinance Lending to Micro and Small Enterprises, 2006

	Number of loans	Outstanding loans (millions of taka)
ASA	215,126	3,126
BRAC	87,272	4,064
Grameen Bank	—	5,872
PKSF and partner MFIs	73,869	757
Total	376,267	13,819

Source: ASA, BRAC, Grameen Bank, and PKSF data.
Note: Data for ASA are as of June 2006 and are for both small business and small entrepreneur loan products, BRAC data are as of April 2006, Grameen data are as of March 2007, and PKSF and partner data are of December 2006. — = not available.

Table 1.10. Microfinance Lending to Marginal and Small Farmers, 2006

	Outstanding loans of PKSF to MFIs (millions of taka)	Outstanding loans of MFIs to clients (millions of taka)	Number of loans
Microfinance for marginal and small farmers	338	329	56,182
Seasonal loans	241	243	22,955
Total	579	572	79,137

Source: PKSF data.
Note: Data for the Microfinance for Marginal and Small Farmers Program are as of December 2006, while data for the Seasonal Loans Program are as of October 2006.

that bank lending to both urban and rural MSMEs accounted for just 2 percent of total lending in 2005.[16]

The microfinance sector—traditionally the largest provider of small loans in rural areas—has stayed focused on the landless poor using group loans and weekly repayments. Such products are not suitable for MSMEs and MSMFs. Only in recent years have some MFIs started targeting the missing middle, in response to demand for larger loans from existing clients.

In 2006, 11 percent of loans from MFIs (by volume) went to enterprises. Enterprise loans ranged from 20,000–500,000 taka, though most were for 20,000–50,000 taka and had a maturity of six months to two years. The pioneer in this segment is BRAC, which in 1996 launched the Micro Enterprise Lending and Assistance (MELA) program. Since then other large MFIs (such as ASA) and up to 100 smaller ones with loans from the PKSF have launched this type of credit product (table 1.9).

Although microfinance lending to enterprises (especially small ones) is limited, microfinance lending to MSMFs is almost irrelevant. In 2006 only 1 percent of microfinance lending (by volume) was disbursed to such farmers, for a total of 79,000 loans (table 1.10).[17] Although some traditional microfinance lending might be extended to or contribute to households borrowing for crops, most is not targeted at MSMFs. This is mainly because most MFIs limit their lending to households that own less than 0.5 acre of land, which excludes MSMFs.

Notes

1. Most of the analysis in this chapter is based on data from Bangladesh Bank. The Bangladeshi financial year ends on 30 June for state banks and on 31 December for private banks. Most of the data in this chapter refer to the 30 June financial year. When data for private and state banks are presented together, they are combined to produce figures for the years concerned.

2. For statistical purposes, Bangladesh Bank treats Grameen Bank as a microfinance institution. This report uses the same designation throughout and so excludes Grameen from bank statistics.

3. The percentages in this sentence are based on data as of December 2005, while the absolute numbers are as of June 2005.

4. Board members are senior civil servants, most of whom lack the skills and time required for effective governance.

5. The most recent waiver was announced in early 2007.

6. According to Bangladesh Bank, this is true for 5 of 30 private commercial banks.

7. As discussed in chapter 3, for example, BKB and RAKUB cover up the extent of their loan portfolio problems by booking credit losses in "other assets" and "investments" accounts.

8. Bangladesh Bank also manages the Small Enterprise Fund, a refinance facility for small enterprises. This facility is not discussed here because it provides loans only to small urban businesses.

9. BKB's most recent board of directors included representatives of the Ministry of Finance, Telecom and Telephone Board, Ministry of Fisheries and Livestock, Bangladesh Rural Development Board (the government's microfinance program), Bangladesh Army, Ministry of Water Resource, Ministry of Establishment, Ministry of Agriculture, and BKB management. Members of RAKUB's most recent board of directors included representatives of the Ministry of Finance, Ministry of Agriculture, Rajshahi district, and RAKUB management.

10. Loanable funds equal 65 percent of the bank's customer deposits, 90 percent of its total deposits, and 100 percent of its equity. Because there are different definitions of small businesses in Bangladesh (see appendix 1), BASIC bank has adopted the Small and Medium Size Enterprise Definition of the Ministry of Industry for manufacturing businesses and the definition of Small and Medium Size Enterprise of Bangladesh Bank for nonmanufacturing enterprises.

11. The second system is referred to also as the "Comilla Model," from the name of the town where this approach was piloted by the Bangladesh Academy for Rural Development.

12. In June 2005 an estimated 71 percent of outstanding loans from RAKUB and 61 percent from BKB were financed by the agriculture refinance facility and 90-day demand facility.

13. Interest waivers apply to BKB and RAKUB as well as nationalized commercial banks. But this report focuses only on BKB and RAKUB, because the others are being privatized and corporatized.

14. In an effort to get some cash, BKB and RAKUB recently implemented a recovery program. The program is technically a rollover of the existing loan portfolio, because borrowers are required to pay only the interest on their loans, but the loans are recorded and provisioned as new performing loans.

15. The only exception is Delta Life Insurance Company, which offers a micro life insurance policy that is very popular in rural areas.

16. Although there is no international benchmark for such lending, 2 percent seems low given that Bangladesh Bank estimates that enterprises with fewer than 10 employees (most of which would be considered micro, small, and medium-size enterprises as defined here) account for an estimated 87 of GDP.

17. This is mainly the result of a recent program sponsored by the International Fund for Agricultural Development and implemented by PKSF partner organizations. None of the three largest microfinance institutions (Grameen Bank, BRAC, and ASA) offers these specialized products to marginal, small and medium-size farmers.

CHAPTER 2

The Missing Middle: Demand-Side Evidence

This chapter discusses sources of finance for Bangladesh's "missing middle"—that is, MSMEs and MSMFs. It also estimates the potential size of the rural market for both, in terms of number of borrowers and volume of credit.

To complement the broad picture of rural access provided by the supply indicators in chapter 1, this chapter measures access from the demand side. The data presented here are from the 2006 Rural MSMEs Finance Survey and from the 2002 Agricultural Credit Survey by Khalily and others. Because the two surveys were among the first attempts to comprehensively measure rural access to financial services for MSMEs and MSMFs, it is not possible to provide comparisons with earlier periods.

The 2006 survey covered 226 MSMEs in the Rajshahi and Moulvibazar districts (see appendix 3 for details on the survey's building blocks, methodology, and sampling),[1] while the 2002 survey covered 806 farmers in all districts.[2]

Access to Credit for MSMEs

In 2006, 43 percent of sampled MSMEs had an account in a bank; among these, more that 90 percent saved in their accounts. Savings averaged 67,000 taka for microenterprises and 90,000 taka for small enterprises.[3] In addition, three-quarters of all the enterprises used banks regularly to make domestic transfers.

Despite the widespread use of bank services, during 2003–06 only 32 percent of MSMEs borrowed from banks (table 2.1). During the same period 16 percent borrowed from MFIs and 8 percent from informal sources (mainly family and friends)—while 44 percent did not borrow at all. Small enterprises borrowed significantly more from banks than did microenterprises.

Micro, small, and medium-size enterprises financed 88 percent of their working capital needs using retained earnings and internal funds, and only 33 percent of new investments were financed using any type of debt. Thus, instead of borrowing, most MSMEs do not try to expand their activities until they have built up internal resources. This pattern is confirmed by their low ratios of debt to assets; this ratio is 2 percent for microenterprises and 20 percent for small businesses, for an average of about 8 percent.[4]

These enterprises do not seem excluded from financial markets due to poor financial performance. Indeed, such enterprises have strong returns on capital (table 2.2) and robust long-term profitability (table 2.3). Instead, many MSMEs seem excluded from financial markets because there is a gap in the market and because lending requirements are not adapted to the business needs of this segment. When borrowing from banks, the average loan for such enterprises is 400,000 taka—while their average loan from MFIs is 38,000 taka (table 2.4).

Table 2.1. Sources of Credit for MSMEs, 2003–06

(percent of total credit)

Type of credit	Micro	Small	Average
Formal	37	77	48
Bank	25	71	32
Microfinance institution	12	6	16
Informal	6	9	8
None	57	14	44

Source: 2006 Rural MSME Finance Survey.

Table 2.2. Returns on Capital for Small and Medium-Size Enterprices, 2005

(percent)

	Return
Small	33
Medium	13
Average	15

Source: SEDF 2006.

Table 2.3. Profitability Measures for Small and Medium-Size Enterprises, 2005
(percent)

	2004	Average, 2002–04
Gross margin	24	23
Operating margin	13	12
Return on invested capital	15	n.a.

Source: SEDF 2006.

Table 2.4. Average Loan Size for MSMEs, 2003–06
(taka)

Loan source	Micro	Small	Average
Bank	169,459	590,588	408,081
Microfinance institution	26,000	75,000	38,250
Informal	43,500	43,750	38,929

Source: 2006 Rural MSME Finance Survey.

Table 2.5. Average Lending Terms from Banks, Microfinance Institutions, and Family and Friends

Indicator	Banks	Microfinance institutions	Family and friends
Processing time (days)	40.4	28.0	5.0
Annual interest rate (percent)	13.6	16.4	14.8
Collateral requirements (value of collateral as percentage of loan)	311.4	56.3	0

Source: 2006 Rural MSME Finance Survey.
Note: It is better to consider average (mean) values than median values because they give a clearer picture of the impact from an institution's perspective.

Getting a loan from formal sources, especially banks, is a long process. Once all the required documents have been submitted, it takes an average of 40 days to get a loan from a bank and 28 days from a MFI (table 2.5).

Banks also require considerable collateral. This requirement partly reflects the difficulties that banks face in repossessing collateral and the fact that borrowers rarely consider discounted asset values. In addition, banks almost exclusively require immovable assets as collateral, while MSMEs have mainly movable assets (figure 2.1).

When asked their top reason for not applying for credit, 40 percent of these enterprises cited the high costs, direct and indirect (table 2.6). Direct costs include both interest rates and other transaction costs (such as for required documents, including financial statements, titles, and the like). Indirect costs include the long wait to get the money (which translates into missed business opportunities) and an intensive application

Figure 2.1. Collateral Requirements of Banks and Assets of MSMEs

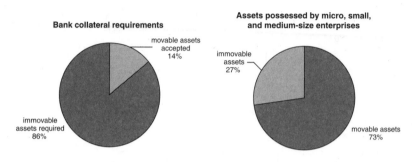

Source: World Bank 2002.

Table 2.6. Top Reasons MSMEs Do Not Apply for Credit

Reason	Percentage of firms citing
High direct and indirect costs	40
Don't need credit	28
Excessive collateral requirements	11
High risks—uncertain of ability to repay debt	6
Other	15

Source: 2006 Rural MSME Finance Survey.

process requiring many meetings between borrowers and banks (again translating into missed opportunities, because of the time spent away from the business). Focus group discussions with MSMEs have found that direct costs equal 6–8 percent of loan values.

The market size for loans to MSMEs is estimated to be nearly 400 billion taka, with 1 million potential clients (box 2.1).

Access to Credit for MSMFs

When considering all types of farmers, almost equal proportions have no access to credit, access only to formal credit (from banks or MFIs), access only to informal sources, and access to both formal and informal sources (table 2.7). Larger farmers are less exclusively dependent on informal sources (15 percent of large farmers compared with 26 percent of the landless) and have better access to credit (just 17 percent of large farmers have no access to credit, compared with 33 percent of the landless). Except for the landless, access to formal credit is almost evenly distributed. Finally, access to both formal and informal credit sources, though common for most types of farmers, is more common among large farmers.

Box 2.1

How Big Is the Potential Market for Providing Credit to MSMEs?

The market size for loans to MSMEs is estimated to be nearly 400 billion taka, with 1 million potential clients (see the table). By comparison, in 2005 total outstanding loans for banks in Bangladesh were 1,117 billion taka.

The estimate of market size is based on the following calculations:

- An estimated 5.9 million micro, small, and medium-size enterprises in 2003—which, based on population growth, suggests 6.8 million such businesses in 2006.
- Only 2.5 million of the 6.8 million enterprises are estimated to have annual profits above 50,000 taka.
- Survey findings indicate that 84 percent of enterprises want to borrow. Of these, only about half will be both willing and able to borrow at a given time (based on the assumption that 70 percent of firms that want to borrow are creditworthy and that 70 percent of these are borrowing at the same time). This means that 1 million micro, small, and medium-size enterprises are potential borrowers.
- About 78 percent of these enterprises are micro, 17 percent small, and 5 percent medium-size.
- The potential lending volume for each segment is calculated by multiplying the number of enterprises in that segment by the average loan for that segment. Average loans are determined by the mean for each segment as defined by this report—for microenterprises, 50,000–300,000 taka; for small, 300,000–1,000,000 taka; and for medium-size, 1–5 million taka. This result assumes that the midpoint of each segment corresponds to the average expected loan for each segment.

Estimated Credit Market for MSMEs

Segment	Share of total (percent)	Number of enterprises	Average loan (taka)	Lending volume (billions of taka)	Market share (percent)
Micro	78	805,477	175,000	140	35
Small	17	179,366	650,000	117	30
Medium	5	46,420	3,000,000	138	35
Total	100	1,031,263		395	100

Source: Authors' calculations based on 2006 Rural MSME Finance Survey, Bangladesh Bank data, and Daniels 2003.

Table 2.7. Borrowing Patterns of Farmers, 2000–02

(percent)

Type of farmer	Size of farm (acres)	No credit	Access to only formal credit (banks and MFIs)	Access to only informal credit	Access to formal and informal credit
Landless	Landless	33.33	18.52	25.93	22.21
	Up to 0.5	24.64	26.57	28.5	20.29
Marginal and small	0.5–2.5	25.62	26.48	19.56	28.38
Medium	2.5–5.0	34.31	30.66	13.87	21.17
	5.0–7.5	40	12	24	24
Large	7.5+	17.2	29.79	14.89	38.3
Total		27.05	26.67	20.97	25.31

Source: Khalily and others 2002.

The biggest anomaly in these data is among medium-size farmers—especially those with 5.0–7.5 acres of land, who have the worst access to credit. Only 12 percent of these farmers have access to formal credit (the lowest share among all the farmer groups), and 40 percent have no access to any credit (the largest share among the groups). Like MSMEs, medium-size farmers seem to build up their equity before trying to expand.

Among farmers with access to formal credit, MFIs focus on the landless while banks focus on medium-size and large farmers (table 2.8). Probably using bank loans to top up their loans from MFIs, 20 percent of marginal and small farmers borrow from both banks and MFIs.

Not surprisingly, the average size of bank loans to farmers increases with farm size (table 2.9). But the average loan per acre declines with increasing farm acreage, and is much lower per acre than loans offered by PKSF's partner organizations participating in its Seasonal Loan Program (9,000 taka an acre). In line with this, farmers that use both bank and informal loans borrow less from banks (though in the range of what those borrowing only from banks do) than from informal sources. In other words, farmers seem to be topping up what they borrow from banks with larger amounts from informal sources. Similarly, informal borrowing grows with farm size. All this seems to indicate that the loan amounts offered by banks are not appropriate, especially for the largest farms.[5]

Although the annual interest rates advertised by banks range from 8–12 percent, the real cost of borrowing from banks is much higher for

Table 2.8. Borrowing Patterns of Farmers with Access to Formal Credit, 2000–02

(percent)

Type of farmer	Size of farm (acres)	Access to only banks	Access to only MFIs	Access to banks and MFIs
Landless	Landless	18.18	72.73	9.09
	Up to 0.5	29.90	55.67	14.43
Small and marginal	0.5–2.5	60.30	20.10	19.60
Medium	2.5–5.0	81.69	8.45	9.86
	5.0–7.5	88.89	11.11	0.00
Large	7.5+	81.25	6.25	12.50
Total		58.00	26.49	15.51

Source: Khalily and others 2002.

Table 2.9. Average Size of Most Recent Loan Taken by Farmers, 2000–02

(taka)

Type of farmer	Size of farm (acres)	Access to only informal sources	Access to only bank sources	Access to both informal and bank sources	
				Informal	Banks
Landless	Landless	25,471	n.a.	8,000	2,500
	Up to 0.5	9,127	4,938	6,585	3,385
Marginal and small	0.5–2.5	18,681	6,327	11,461	5,020
Medium	2.5–5.0	17,752	10,157	15,550	6,525
	5.0–7.5	13,833	13,333	5,040	10,300
Large	7.5+	79,428	16,461	28,715	14,423

Source: Khalily and others 2002.
Note: n.a. = not applicable.

Table 2.10. Transaction Costs of Most Recent Loan Taken by Farmers, 2000–02

Type of farmer	Size of farm (acres)	Cost (percentage of loan principal)
Landless	Landless	42.98
	Up to 0.5	14.48
Marginal and small	0.5–2.5	10.14
Medium	2.5–5.0	9.52
	5.0–7.5	3.42
Large	7.5+	7.7
Total		13.36

Source: Khalily and others 2002.

Box 2.2

How Big Is the Potential Market for Providing Credit to MSMFs?

The market size for loans to MSMFs is estimated to be nearly 88 billion taka, with 4.3 million potential clients (see the box table). By comparison, in 2005 banks in Bangladesh disbursed 42 billion taka for crop production loans. (The disbursed amount is reported rather than the outstanding amount because the latter includes a large share of overdue loans that should be written off, and because most crop loans are annual anyway.)

The estimate of market size is based on the following calculations:

- The average farm size for each segment was calculated as the midpoint acreage in each segment.
- Farm credit requirements were estimated at 9,000 taka per acre, which is the same amount used by PKSF in its Seasonal Loan Program.
- The number of farmers willing and able to borrow was calculated by taking the total number of farmers from the 1996/97 Agricultural Census (though the population has grown since then, the proportion of people working in agriculture is decreasing and agricultural land has not increased), then discounting the number by 50 percent for each farmer segment (based on the assumption that 70 percent of those who want to borrow are creditworthy and that 70 percent of these are borrowing at the same time).
- The potential demand from each segment was calculated by multiplying the average farm size in that segment by estimated loan size per acre and the estimated number of potential borrowers.

Estimated Credit Market for MSMFs

Segment	Average farm size (acres)	Loan size per acre	Number of farmers (millions)	Lending volume (billions of taka)	Market share (percent)
Marginal (0.5–1.49 acres)	1	9,000	2.2	20	23
Small (1.5–2.5 acres)	2	9,000	1.0	18	20
Medium (2.5–7.5 acres)	5	9,000	1.1	50	57
Total			4.3	88	100

Source: Authors' calculations based on the 1996/97 Agricultural Census and PKSF data.

farmers—on average, 13 percentage points higher (table 2.10). These additional transaction costs mainly involve bribes, costs of required documents, and transportation costs to reach banks. Transaction costs fall as farm size increases, because large farmers usually possess what banks need to assess their creditworthiness (such as formal documents).[6]

The market size for loans to MSMFs is estimated to be nearly 88 billion taka, with 4.3 million potential clients (box 2.2).

Notes

1. Although the sample included 226 enterprises, 37 had an annual profit below 50,000 taka. Thus they are not included in the analysis here because they do not fit the definition of MSME used in this report.

2. See chapter 2 of Khalily and others (2002) for details on the survey's methodology and sampling.

3. Only seven medium-size businesses were included in the survey, so they are not listed in separate categories in the discussion in this section. But averages for the entire sample in the text and tables based on the survey include MSMEs.

4. By comparison, in many developing countries this share is 30-40 percent.

5. That banks offer loans that are too small may explain why large farmers with access only to informal sources borrow extremely large amounts. That landless farmers in the same position also borrow large amounts from the informal sector could not be explained and probably is not representative of the category, as there are only seven observations in the sample.

6. Although it is not surprising that the transaction costs of borrowing from the formal sector are highest for landless farmers, it should be highlighted that the sample contains very few observations of landless with access to formal credit. Hence the number may not be representative.

CHAPTER 3

Constraints on Increasing Access to Finance for the Missing Middle

This chapter examines the legal, regulatory, and institutional constraints that a critical group of financial institutions—BKB, RAKUB, private banks, and MFIs—face in providing financial services to rural MSMEs and MSMFs. It also analyzes the constraints that traditional, multiperil crop insurance schemes face when serving such farmers. The analysis is based on data from chapters 1 and 2 and case studies of two banks (and detailed discussions with others) and six MFIs.

Despite extensive efforts by Bangladesh's government, access to finance in rural areas remains limited—especially for MSMEs and MSMFs.

BKB and RAKUB, which are supposed to be the primary providers of financial services in rural areas, are deeply insolvent. Bangladesh Bank's refinance facility, designed to facilitate agricultural lending, has instead become the main source of funding for BKB and RAKUB's growing operating losses, and agricultural lending is falling as a share of total lending. This situation has severely compromised the two banks' capacity to serve the missing middle.

Other potential sources of rural finance, such as private banks, earn enough from corporate lending that they have limited incentives to expand in rural areas. Although required to open one rural branch for every four opened in urban areas, rural branches opened by private banks are mainly used to collect deposits that are then used for loans in urban rather than rural areas. Most lending opportunities in rural areas involve MSMEs and MSMFs—which banks cannot serve profitably under the current legal and regulatory framework and the constraints imposed by current lending technologies. Although lending profitably to such enterprises is not easy, doing so for such farmers is even more challenging because of the difficulties that agricultural lending presents, including weather risks, limited financial capacity among rural households, lack of distribution channels, low unit size of transactions, and high operating costs. Finally, while MFIs operate in rural areas, they focus on the landless and do not have appropriate lending methodologies to serve larger, more complex clients.

Although a variety of financial institutions (such as BRDB and BSBL) serve rural areas, this chapter focuses on the most critical subset of institutions for three reasons. First, the institutions analyzed here are the largest rural lenders in terms of loan volumes—BKB accounts for 13 percent of rural lending, RAKUB for 5 percent, private banks for 22 percent, and MFIs for 20 percent. Only nationalized commercial banks have a larger lending volume, and they are not analyzed here because they are being privatized (or in the case of Sonali Bank, corporatized). Second, BKB, RAKUB, and private banks have large rural deposit portfolios, so their financial health can affect the stability of the entire rural system. Third, BKB and RAKUB are the main cause of distortions in rural financial markets due to their importance and the government policies to which they are subjected (such as interest rate caps and waivers of principal and interest after natural disasters and before elections).

BKB's and RAKUB's Deep Insolvency

BKB and RAKUB are the largest providers of financial services in rural areas. In 2005 they accounted for 28 percent of bank branches, 23 percent of outstanding bank loans (by volume), and 8 percent of bank deposits (by volume) in rural areas. But as noted, both banks suffer from increasingly severe liquidity constraints.

The banks' financial distress is driven by politically influenced governance and weak internal operating, accounting, and control systems. Politically influenced governance has led to repeated waivers of interest, and sometimes principal, on small agricultural loans (less than 5,000 taka) after natural disasters and before elections. These waivers—and a lack of government compensation for them—generate a vicious circle that makes lending unprofitable for the two banks.[1] This happens because the banks' already low interest income on such loans falls by a quarter or half (depending on the waiver),[2] and even the partial compensation due to the banks for waivers is never actually paid by the government. Moreover, the waivers create a culture of nonrepayment among other clients, who also feel entitled not to make loan payments.

Finally, the large amount of overdue loans accumulated over time has made both banks entirely dependent on the agricultural refinance facility for liquidity and cash with which to pay their operating expenses. (Their deposits have been used to fund old nonperforming loans, and their operating cash flows are deeply negative.) This makes the banks' loan portfolios more exposed to waivers, which are provided only for agricultural loans, for which the refinance facility is used.

Despite efforts by BKB's management, the bank's condition continued to deteriorate between July 2004 and June 2005, and the scale of its insolvency is such that the bank cannot solve its problems using its own resources. Continued growth in the bank's loan portfolio appears simply to be driving up losses, with the regulatory capital shortfall growing at about the same rate as the portfolio. Moreover, the total capital shortfall grew at about twice that rate, reaching 26 billion taka in 2005 (table 3.1).

Despite a capital injection of 420 million taka in 2004, RAKUB reported negative capital in 2005 (table 3.2). The total regulatory capital shortfall identified by its auditors rose to 2.3 billion taka due to extremely negative net income, driven by excessive operating costs and low net interest income, and despite the fact that the bank again reversed provisions against its classified loans in 2005.

Although the performance of BKB and RAKUB as indicated by their audited statements is very poor, their actual performance is likely to be much worse. First, in addition to reported losses, both banks' balance sheets include large amounts of questionable items booked as good assets. These include accumulated credit losses (some more than 11 years old), booked as "other assets" in anticipation of compensation from the government, that have not been provisioned for or written off and that are unlikely to be repaid.

Second, the fact that interest income on nonperforming loans is being recorded as accrued interest (rather than being suspended, as it

Table 3.1. Selected Data from BKB's Audited Balance Sheet, 2004–05

Item	Millions of taka		Change (percent)
	2004	2005	
Total assets	87,417	95,284	9.0
Total loans	59,793	65,675	9.8
Total deposits	49,982	56,344	12.7
Borrowings from Bangladesh Bank	30,951	33,389	7.9
Reported capital	−14,101	−15,519	10.1
Regulatory capital shortfall	−20,275	−22,278	9.9
Additional provisions identified by auditors	−1,745	−3,711	112.6
Total capital shortfall identified by auditors	−22,020	−25,989	18.0
Adjusted capital/total assets (percent)	−16	−16	0
Borrowings from Bangladesh Bank/total assets (percent)	35	35	0
Gross loans and advances	59,793	65,674	9.8
Gross unclassified loans and advances	35,418	40,885	15.4
Gross classified loans and advances	24,375	24,789	1.7
Net loans/total assets (percent)	68	69	0
Net loans/deposits (percent)	120	117	0
Gross classified loans/gross loans (percent)	41	38	0

Source: BKB audited financial statements 2004–05.
Note: The regulatory capital shortfall is calculated using the bank's audited balance sheet (that is, before adjusting for underprovisioning of loan losses and overreporting of income), while the total capital shortfall identified by auditors takes into account identified (but not taken) additional provisions, but not overreporting of income.

should be) reflects the banks' lack of effective governance, accounting, management, control, loan administration, internal audit, risk control, and risk assessment systems.[3]

Finally, the quality of auditing is dubious at both banks. BKB auditors sign off on financial statements that they acknowledge present a completely inaccurate picture of the bank's condition (and, under international auditing guidelines, would likely require the auditors to express a negative opinion on BKB's viability as a going concern)—reflecting low auditing standards. Similarly, despite improvements in 2005, RAKUB's audit report was also weak and failed to appropriately address the significant problems of capital, earnings, and systems that it identifies. In particular, the bank's auditors identified its weak systems as a major cause of poor financial reporting, yet accepted the bank's books more or less as is. Most troublesome was that the auditors allowed to pass without comment the bank's low level of provisions (amounting to about 26 percent of classified loans and 8 percent of all loans) and practice of reversing them to generate "earnings."

Table 3.2. Selected Data from RAKUB'S Audited Balance Sheet, 2004–05

Item	Millions of taka		Change (percent)
	2004	2005	
Total assets	27,989	30,386	8.6
Total loans	18,327	21,428	16.9
Total deposits	10,807	11,579	7.1
Borrowings from Bangladesh Bank	13,402	15,607	16.5
Reported capital	268	−98	
Regulatory capital shortfall	−1,904	−2,271	19.2
Additional provisions identified by auditors	0	−4	0.0
Total capital shortfall identified by auditors	−1,904	−2,275	19.4
Adjusted capital/total assets (percent)	−7	−7	0
Borrowings from Bangladesh Bank/total assets (percent)	48	51	0
Gross loans and advances	18,327	21,428	16.9
Gross unclassified loans and advances	11,025	15,020	36.2
Gross classified loans and advances	7,302	6,407	−12.2
Net loans/total assets (percent)	65	71	0
Net loans/deposits (percent)	170	185	0
Gross classified loans/gross loans (percent)	40	30	0

Source: RAKUB audited financial statements 2004–05.
Note: The regulatory capital shortfall is calculated using the bank's audited balance sheet (that is, before adjusting for underprovisioning of loan losses and overreporting of income), while the total capital shortfall identified by auditors takes into account identified (but not taken) additional provisions, but not overreporting of income.

Once their loan portfolios have been fully provisioned for losses, and worthless assets written off, the real losses of the banks are estimated at 51–61 billion taka for BKB and 12–16 billion taka for RAKUB. (Appendix 4 provides detailed estimates for both banks, including the assumptions underlying these estimates.) As deeply insolvent institutions, neither BKB nor RAKUB is in a position to scale up lending to the missing middle.

Challenges for Private Banks

Although private banks have been increasing lending in rural areas, it remains limited. This is mainly because in rural areas most potential bank clients are MSMEs and MSMFs, which have very different features from large corporations—the traditional clients of private banks—which are easier to serve profitably. Despite the challenges that MSMEs present (including low-value transactions, limited formality, and sensitivity to loan delivery time), lending to farmers presents even more obstacles (including exposure to weather risks). This section focuses on the obstacles that banks face in serving smaller enterprises as well as the additional challenges of targeting smaller farmers. In addition, the section on insurance below discusses how risk transfer mechanisms could be developed to facilitate agricultural lending.

Micro, small, and medium-size enterprises are usually family businesses, run and managed by one or two people who take full responsibility for all aspects of the business. Although these individuals typically know their business, they are often weak at producing written business and financial plans and are discouraged by the documentation requirements of banks. Moreover, management rarely plans operations far in advance—so when such enterprises require financing, they usually need it immediately. These enterprises usually have limited financial statements and few immovable assets. Business and household finances are often strongly intertwined, and such businesses work mainly with cash—that is, they deposit only part of their revenues in banks.

Finally, the banking needs of MSMEs are unlike those of large corporations, and even among these enterprises product preferences differ considerably. Focus group discussions with MSMEs found that they placed varying importance on interest rates, loan processing times, collateral requirements, and transaction costs. The smaller the enterprise, the more sensitive the borrower becomes to loan processing times and collateral requirements, and the less sensitive to interest rates (table 3.3).

To profitably serve MSMEs, banks need to minimize transaction costs and generate a large number of high-quality loans. As in similar activities with small profit margins, banks need to increase revenue by making many loans while lowering expenses—for example, by making loan officers more productive and avoiding bad loans.

For several reasons, banks in Bangladesh find it difficult to serve MSMEs profitably. First, the legal and regulatory framework (especially rules on provisioning, credit bureau reporting, and movable collateral) makes it expensive to serve this market segment. Second, when lending, banks make little or no distinction between large corporations and smaller enterprises in terms of the products they offer or the demands and

Table 3.3. Differing Loan Product Preferences for MSMEs

Product criteria	Relative importance	
	Micro loans	Small loans
Interest rates	Low	High
Loan processing time	High	Low
Collateral requirements	High	Low
Transaction costs	High	Low

Source: Focus group discussions with MSMEs.

procedures they apply. Third, banks do not segment MSMEs. Finally, banks do not have organizational structures and monitoring tools conducive to achieving high efficiency.

Legal and regulatory framework

Bangladesh's provisioning rules make lending to MSMEs more expensive than other types of lending. First, general loan loss provisioning for these enterprises is 2 percent, instead of the 1 percent applied to consumer loans and SBLs refinanced under Bangladesh Bank's facility for small and medium-size enterprises (Bangladesh Bank 2006b). In addition to raising the cost of lending to MSMEs—for no reason[4]—this requirement discriminates against banks that make such loans using their own funds, by giving preferential treatment to banks that use the refinance facility.

Second, Bangladesh Bank's provisioning rules require that the amount provisioned be calculated as the overdue loan amount minus the discounted value of selected collateral. Selected collateral includes immovable assets and only movable assets that are fully controlled by the bank, making it impossible for MSMEs to pledge assets that they need for daily operations. Hence if such an enterprise has neither immovable property nor movable assets that can be given up for bank possession, lending to it is more expensive because the base for calculating provisioning is higher.

Although provisioning requirements for MSMEs are too stringent, overall provisioning rules are too lax and do not create the right incentives for careful monitoring. Specifically, term loans for less than five years are classified based on the criteria listed in figure 3.1.[5] Given that banks need to test the repayment capacity of previously unbanked clients and that to make small business lending profitable the portfolio

Figure 3.1. Classification Criteria for Term Loans of Less than Five Years

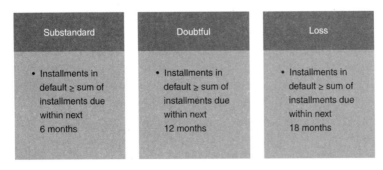

Substandard	Doubtful	Loss
• Installments in default ≥ sum of installments due within next 6 months	• Installments in default ≥ sum of installments due within next 12 months	• Installments in default ≥ sum of installments due within next 18 months

at risk above 30 days has to be low, current provisioning requirements could lead banks to undertake lax supervision of loans to MSMEs.

Bangladesh's credit bureau takes a long time to generate reports— usually 7–10 working days—which slows growth in loans to MSMEs. Moreover, the information provided on such loans is outdated because bank reporting on loans of 50,000–10 million taka is done only quarterly. The information provided is also limited. For example, other outstanding loans and guarantees provided by borrowers are not recorded, and only information for the current month is reported. Although the fact that the credit bureau provides outdated and partial information is a problem for lending in general, the issue is more serious for lending to smaller enterprises. The lack of timely, accurate information on these enterprises is a bigger concern due to their limited credit history, less accurate statements, and lower formality.

Finally, though not compulsory, Bangladesh Bank's regulations on small enterprise financing (which also cover medium-size enterprises) do not facilitate lending to MSMEs. First, the recommended organizational structure requires that banks split loan sales from monitoring—an approach that does not facilitate in-depth client knowledge, which is crucial in this market.[6] Second, the policy requires that loans be reviewed by a special unit, slowing the growth of lending to MSMEs.[7]

Such enterprises have limited immovable collateral but a wide array of movable assets (see chapter 2). Yet Bangladesh's legal framework on movable property precludes these assets from being used productively in loan contracts, making these assets dead capital.

A well-functioning regime for secured transactions is based on the following related principles:

- Creation of security interests over movable assets is easy and allowed on most assets and by every entity (both physical and juridical persons).
- Priority rankings are clearly defined among those who might have claims on property offered as collateral.
- There is a place (such as a registry) for making priority interests publicly known.
- Enforcement of security interests for all assets is fast and cheap. Though this is important for all types of property, it is particularly so for movable assets subject to rapid depreciation.

The current framework for movable collateral has major deficiencies that limit businesses' ability to use movable assets as collateral.[8] The fact that most MSMEs are sole proprietorships makes this an even bigger problem. Appendix 5 presents a detailed analysis of the secured transactions regime and its shortcomings. The system's main deficiencies are:

- *Legal provisions that determine priority among types of creditors, continuations of proceeds, and modifications to charges are unclear.*[9] Different security interest laws have different priority structures, creating confusion about the order of priority and so increasing lenders' risk of loss and reducing the leverage value of property used as collateral. The system permits a security interest to continue in proceeds only in a limited way. For example, if the security interest is an intermediary input, such as cotton, the security interest no longer applies once the cotton is transformed into a garment. In addition, Bangladesh has no clear priority rules for future advances or modifications to a registered charge. Such advances or modifications could include increasing the amount secured or adding new parties to the charge. As a result taking assets as security is risky, because lenders never know where they stand in the priority structure.
- *Only corporations creating certain types of security interests can register them in the Registrar of Joint Stock Companies and Firms.*[10] This approach heavily discriminates against MSMEs (as well as MSMFs), most of which are not set up as corporate entities and so are not registered at the registry, and which own mainly movable assets. Moreover, the fact that some interests are not registered makes the registration system ineffective. In addition, for movable property attached in some way to immovable property, there is only case law that the intention of the landowner and occupier determines whether the property will remain the property of the occupier—and not form part of the "land"—and so be considered movable property. This affects lending against fixtures such as generators, machinery installed on property, and certain temporary structures.
- *The transaction costs of filing security agreements are high.* First, given the registry's low capacity, firms often must use facilitators to ensure that registration occurs—both because the process is long and because facilitators know how to expedite it. Second, because the registry is paper-based, verifying collateral is a time-consuming process that does not allow potential lenders to conduct real-time searches of existing liens.[11] This substantially increases the risk of secured lending for lenders, who cannot be sure that the collateral offered by borrowers is unencumbered. Third, laws on evidence require corroboration of any documents

that are not originals and that do not bear an original signature. This means that only "original" evidence is admissible, increasing the cost of filing and, given the state of the registry, making loss of or damage to original documents probable.

- *Enforcement of debt recovery is slow.* Despite the creation of the money loan court to speed up debt recovery for banks and financial interme- diaries regulated by Bangladesh Bank, enforcement takes one to three years—by which time most movable property will have lost all or most of its value. Although the court must issue a judgment within three months of filing, enforcing a judgment requires filing an execu- tion case. This process makes it difficult for financial institutions to sell collateral because by then the property is usually absent or because such actions are stayed by judicial order due to challenges from debtors. Debtors have wide scope to seek injunctions requiring judi- cial review by the Supreme Court of Bangladesh, and hearings of debt recovery cases are stayed until injunctions have been completed. Moreover, enforcement of orders for repossession is uncertain. This is partly because there is no legislation or procedure for access to, seizure, and sale of secured movable property (except pledges) and partly because enforcement relies on understaffed and undermotivated police—court police officers or ordinary police officers.

Complex, expensive lending procedures and inappropriate products

Bank procedures for lending to MSMEs are too complex for them, mak- ing such lending unnecessarily time consuming and costly for both the banks and the businesses. On average it takes a bank 29 steps, 9 staff, and 50 documents to issue a loan to such an enterprise—leading to a total approval time of 30–80 days once all the documents have been submitted (table 3.4). Such long procedures mean that banks can approve at most

Table 3.4. Application Process for Bank Loans to MSMEs

Indicator	Average number
Steps	29
Meetings with borrower	9
Borrower payments	10
Documents	50
Document length (pages)	200
Staff involved	9
Borrower time (hours)	20

Source: Authors' calculations.

3–4 loans a month per loan officer. For banks to make a profit serving such enterprises, under current cost structures, each loan officer would have to make at least 8–10 loans a month.

Enterprises seeking bank loans must attend an average of nine meetings, taking 20 hours. This translates into missed business opportunities for MSMEs both because it takes a long time to get loans and because the owner or manager (and often one of the few employees) must spend time away from the business. In addition, borrowing from banks involves high transaction costs beyond interest payments (see also chapter 2). For a 300,000 taka loan the borrower must pay, on average, an additional 6.6 percent for legal fees, collateral registration, and documentation (such as preparation of financial statements, business plan, title, and the like; figure 3.2).

Because of the weak framework for movable collateral, banks require immovable assets as collateral (except BRAC Bank; see box 3.1). Yet MSMEs have mostly movable assets. Finally, banks mainly provide continuous credit products to these enterprises, which restricts the banks' pool of such clients. Continuous credit products are more risky for clients that are often unbanked and that rarely deposit their revenues in banks; hence banks often require that MSMEs have deposit accounts for a few months before they will extend loans to them.

Figure 3.2. Transaction Costs on a 12-Month, 300,000 Taka Bank Loan

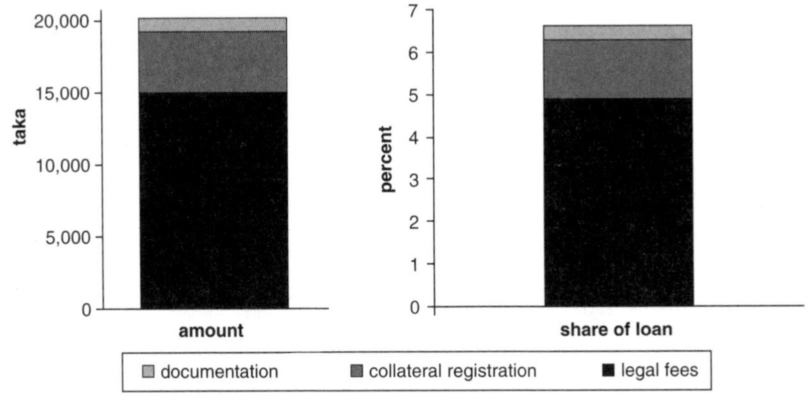

Source: Authors' calculations.

Box 3.1

BRAC Bank—Serving MSMEs

BRAC Bank is possibly the only bank in Bangladesh that focuses on MSMEs. BRAC Bank was founded in 2001 by BRAC (a nongovernmental organization), the International Finance Corporation, and Shorecap. By 2006 it had 200,000 deposit accounts and 45,000 loan accounts. The average loan was 28,000 taka, while portfolio at risk above 30 days was 6 percent. The bank has 22 branches, 350 unit offices, and 19 automated teller machines (ATMs) across the country. The unit offices only market loans, which are approved at the bank's branches or headquarters.

BRAC Bank has developed six products for micro, small, and medium-size enterprises. Most loans are secured with movable assets and, for sole proprietors, with postdated checks from borrowers. Since defaulting on a check is a criminal offense, borrowers have a strong incentive to repay loans secured that way.

Although possibly the best approach in the current environment, for several reasons this is an imperfect way to secure loans. First, defaulting borrowers may face criminal offenses—and sending debtors to prison is an archaic, objectionable way of enforcing loan contracts. Second, the amount of the checks used to secure loans cannot be large if they are to be credible for small borrowers. So, while this practice may work for small loans, it will not be enough to ensure that loan sizes are scaled up as enterprises grow. Finally, using postdated checks means that loans are still provisioned as unsecured loans, resulting in higher provisioning requirements.

Lack of market segmentation

Most commercial banks engage in little segmentation and simply lump all MSMEs into one group, ignoring differences in the market (again, except for BRAC Bank). But as noted, and as highlighted in focus group discussions, there are significant differences among these enterprises.[12]

Limited specialization and no measures of small business performance

As in other business activities involving low-value transactions, efficiency is crucial when lending to MSMEs. To achieve high efficiency, specialization of staff, training, and procedures is essential. Yet most banks in Bangladesh do not have specialized loan officers, training, and procedures for such lending.

To increase efficiency, this type of lending needs to be measured and staff incentives aligned accordingly. Although banks in Bangladesh have sophisticated management information systems, they generally do not use them to monitor the efficiency of individual staff members and lending departments, and staff rewards are usually unrelated to efficiency or the quality of the portfolios they manage.

Additional challenges in serving MSMFs
Banks face additional challenges when lending to MSMFs, including:

- Training loan officers in appraising agricultural activities.
- Developing products with flexible repayment schedules that fit agricultural cycles.
- Coping with weather risks.
- Developing delivery and monitoring mechanisms that keep costs low while serving sparsely populated areas (though due to its high population density, this is less of an issue in Bangladesh than in many other countries).

Challenges for Microfinance Institutions

Although MFIs have started expanding access to the missing middle, their outreach remains limited. To scale up lending to MSMEs and MSMFs, these institutions must address a number of challenges. These market segments require new and bigger loan products, mainly targeted at male borrowers, who want to borrow individually. In addition, such clients often have more complex finances—requiring rigorous financial analysis. All this increases lending costs, making the segment more expensive to serve than traditional microfinance borrowers. Given the larger loans and increased risks involved, MFIs must introduce basic management information systems. Finally, MSMFs are exposed to weather risks and require financing simultaneously, making loans from MFIs more seasonal. (See appendix 6 for a more detailed analysis of lending by selected MFIs to MSMEs and MSMFs.)

Limited numbers of target borrowers
Maintaining low costs requires that lenders locate a sufficient number of creditworthy clients in the market area being served, so that loan officers

specialized in specific market segments can achieve large loan portfolios. Although Bangladesh has a huge number of MSMEs, the number in any given market area may be limited. ASA, for example, had a hard time locating enough small, production-oriented enterprises to meet its goal of 150 borrowers for each of its specialized branches supporting the Small Entrepreneurs Loan program (box 3.2). This situation required a change in strategy, leading to the opening of special windows for this product in ASA's regular branches rather than operating specialized branches. In some areas MFIs may encounter too few potential clients to warrant offering specialized products.

Box 3.2

ASA's Microenterprise Programs

ASA, one of the three largest microfinance institutions in Bangladesh, offers two specialized microenterprise programs: the Small Business Loan program and Small Entrepreneurs Loan program. The Small Business Loan program was launched in 1993 to serve traders, shopkeepers, and graduates of ASA's small loan program. The first cycle of loans ranges from 15,000–50,000 taka, and successive loans are increased by a maximum of 5,000 taka a year. The program uses a group lending methodology, with weekly repayments. The Small Entrepreneurs Loan program, started in 2003, targets production-oriented microenterprises. Loans range from 30,000–200,000 taka, for a maximum of 24 months, with monthly rather than weekly payments.

No collateral is required for either product, but a guarantor is required for the SBLs program. By June 2006 this program had nearly 200,000 loans, with 2.4 billion taka outstanding. At the same date, the Small Entrepreneurs Loan program had issued 15,805 loans worth 723 million taka.

ASA face two challenges in trying to scale up the Small Entrepreneurs Loan program. First, the requirement that such loans be made only to production-oriented businesses limits the universe of potential clients. Second, the fact that ASA does not take physical collateral limits the possibility of increasing the maximum loan size under the program. Moreover, it would be difficult for smaller microfinance institutions to adopt this program model, because they may not have enough capital to offer such large loans or highly skilled loan officers able to estimate cash-flows of potential borrowers.

Serving male borrowers

Most MFIs lend mainly to women, because they are more amenable than men to joining loan groups and attending meetings, accepting responsibility for repaying loans of defaulting group members, and meeting other responsibilities of group membership. The opportunity to leave home and interact with others in weekly or monthly meetings offers a socially accepted reason to leave the confines of the home and helps women build confidence to engage in business activities. In addition, women may be more susceptible than men to pressure from loan officers and other group members to make loan payments on time.

By contrast, crop farming and large-scale trading and production activities are dominated by men. As a result, when lending for such activities, MFIs must decide whether to continue to target women (while knowing that men will be the ones who actually use the loan funds) or, alternatively, adjust their lending approaches to lend directly to the men who operate many farms and MSMEs (box 3.3).

Adjusting lending methodologies

Microfinance institutions in Bangladesh traditionally extend loans that are "secured" using the Grameen Bank's group lending approach. But many MSMEs and MSMFs prefer individual loans. Given the larger loans involved, and from a purely financial perspective, MFIs need to shift to individual loans for larger clients. In fact, only by shifting to individual lending will MFIs be able to analyze individual borrowers and set loan terms and conditions based on the risks they present.

Group members in most MFIs have little liability for loan payments by other group members, though loan officers may urge group leaders to pressure delinquent borrowers to repay. Few MFIs have started shifting to individual loans and different forms of collateral. Making individual loans even at the micro level requires considerable planning and building of institutional capacity, followed by testing, evaluation, and mainstreaming of new products (Dellient and others 2005). These challenges will be even greater if MFIs try to expand lending to farmers.

Small loan sizes and lending for household activities

Microfinance institutions currently focus on seasonal and farm loans oriented to the enterprise, activity, and person being funded. Because farms are small, the demand for loans for a specific crop—especially rice—is small even when improved production techniques are used. Moreover, average farm sizes rarely grow over time, so there is little opportunity for

Box 3.3

BEES's Product for Marginal and Small Farmers

Through 10 of its 83 branches, Bangladesh Extension Education Services (BEES), a microfinance institution, targets marginal and small female farmers. As of 2006 BEES had 11,400 farmer borrowers (or 12 percent of its total borrowers). During the same year it had disbursed 72 million taka in farm loans (equivalent to 13 percent of its disbursements for the year).

These loans are essentially an adaptation of the Grameen Bank's group lending approach applied to agriculture, with women engaged in a variety of agricultural activities as clients. Loans are to be repaid within a year in 45 weekly installments. BEES forms groups of 15–40 women that meet for one hour a week to engage in financial transactions and occasionally receive other services, such as monthly health checkups. Mandatory weekly savings earn an annual interest rate of 5 percent. One percent of the loan is deducted as a premium for micro life insurance and to cover other service expenses.

Although this product has succeeded in increasing lending to small farmers, there are limits on BEES's ability to scale up its lending—in terms of both loan sizes and volumes. To be able to target larger farmers, BEES will have to start lending to men, who are likely to prefer individual loans. Making individual loans requires estimating households' monthly cash flows and evaluating borrowers' repayment capacity. Moreover, BEES's group-based weekly repayment lending approach is not particularly well suited to the seasonality of crop farming.

MFIs to increase loan sizes by lending for individual crops. Relaxing this constraint would require these institutions to develop greater capacity to appraise and lend against the entire portfolio of household economic activities, including all crops and products produced for consumption and sale as well as nonagricultural activities undertaken by all household members who will contribute to loan repayment.

Training loan officers in financial analysis

Microfinance institutions are accustomed to using a Grameen-style methodology to serve clients capable of generating the regular cash flows needed for weekly payments. As a result, microloan portfolios are dominated by borrowers engaged in small-scale trading, poultry, and dairy production. This methodology does not require loan officers to have the advanced skills needed to evaluate borrowers' businesses.

But offering loans for larger crop or livestock operations, or for production loans for nonagricultural activities, requires that loan officers have more business and technical knowledge about the enterprise being financed and the economic subsector involved, as well as greater capacity to evaluate clients, their businesses, and their competition. It also requires that loan officers have a social and economic status approximately equal to their borrowers.

Introducing management information systems and new technology

Loans to MSMEs, whether to graduates of standard microfinance programs or entirely new clients, will by definition be larger on average than traditional microfinance loans. Making larger loans raises the risk of larger losses for MFIs in cases of default. To manage such a portfolio effectively, introducing even a basic management information system, including careful client monitoring, is essential.

The strong profitability of Bangladesh's microfinance is based on their low costs—reflecting, among other things, their low cost of funds, good portfolio quality, and group lending methodology. In particular, group lending has allowed MFIs to generate a high number of borrowers per staff and so low costs per borrower. But serving MSMEs using individual lending requirements, more complex financial analysis, and better-trained staff will be more expensive, and these costs may be only partly offset by larger loan sizes. To keep staff productivity high and costs low, increasing the use of technology may be essential.

Managing liquidity

When serving MSMFs, MFIs must address the liquidity management challenge created by the seasonality of credit demand from farmers. Financing crops implies making a lot of loans at the beginning of the planting season—followed by several months of low or no repayments while crops grow or cattle fatten (unless borrowers have other sources of income). Then at harvest time, borrowers earn income and prefer to repay their loans in lump sums.

The resulting large flow of funds into MFIs may accumulate and then largely sit idle until the start of the next crop or fattening season. Crop lending also introduces seasonality into the workloads of loan officers, so MFIs may need to adjust employee compensation levels, require compulsory furloughs during slack periods, and use improved technology to accelerate data processing.

Addressing weather risks

Weather risk is the main source of income instability for farmers borrowing from MFIs, because their agricultural activities depend on rainfall and access to water for irrigation is limited except in areas where tube wells have been installed. Accordingly, MFIs become financially vulnerable to weather risk as well. Weather-induced crop failures, usually due to low rainfall, often cause overdue repayments on crop term loans—threatening the portfolio quality of MFIs. To address this problem, these institutions should diversify their risks by developing loan portfolios that cover large areas. But most MFIs do not have the opportunity to diversify geographically; hence the importance of agricultural insurance.

Challenges for Insurance Providers Serving MSMFs

In the late 1970s Bangladesh's government designed a multiperil crop insurance scheme that was administered by SBC. The scheme failed because of the standard drawbacks of farm-level, multiperil crop insurance:

- *Adverse selection.* The insurance product was voluntary, but due to limited resources it was offered only in selected, higher-risk *thanas.*
- *Poor due diligence and supervision.* Many farmers insured unproductive land or filed claims when crops had been destroyed by causes other than natural disasters.
- *Weak control over loss assessments.* It proved difficult to assess losses using an objective methodology. A variety of methods was used, including crop cutting and eye estimation, and there were frequent disputes.
- *High administrative costs.*
- *High crop yield guarantee.* The scheme guaranteed 80 percent of expected crop yields, which is high by international standards.[13]
- *Individual farmer insurance.* Insured yields were based on *thana*-level average yields, while losses were adjusted and indemnified based on actual yields on individual farms. This approach exposed the scheme to claims arising from poor management by individual farmers.

This insurance product was—like all traditional crop insurance—more appropriate for large farmers. Such programs rely on examinations of

Table 3.5. Features of Traditional Crop Insurance and Index Insurance

Function	Traditional	Index
Establishing yield of insured	Insurers must establish farm- or district-level yield. **Cost: High**	Payout based solely on the measured index (such as rainfall). **Cost: Low**
Underwriting	Requires assessment of individual or local risk. **Cost: High**	Not required, though insurers need to screen clients for insurable interest (for example, to ensure that the farmer is growing a crop). **Cost: Low**
Policy sales	Sales process requires high skills because it involves underwriting decisions. **Cost: High**	Sales process requires good product knowledge, but no major underwriting decisions occur in the sale process. **Cost: Medium**
Paperwork and technology	Generally complex. Need to record yield history, crop establishment during the season, and farm and field details **Cost: High**	Simple certificates or coupons. **Cost: Medium**
Field inspection	Need to check for emergence of crop. **Cost: High**	Not required. **Cost: Low**
Loss adjustment	Need to inspect crop damage and adjust claims. **Cost: High**	Not required: Payments based on measured index. **Cost: Low**
Claims payment	Settlement of claims. **Cost: Low**	Settlement of claims. **Cost: Low**

individual farms and evaluations of yield, driving up costs considerably. This approach is not suited to serving MSMFs, as this is a low-value transaction business. Costs aside, this type of weather risk management suffers from moral hazard problems—especially for MSMFs, who are less likely to use fertilizers and pesticides. Indeed, when they know they are insured, farmers often take less care of their crops.

Instead, commercially viable approaches to agricultural insurance for low-value transactions are based on the use of objective factors. So-called index insurance relies on an index (such as the amount of rainfall), based on historical events and yields, to set objective triggers that determine if and when there are payouts to farmers (table 3.5). Index-based crop insurance is actuarial-based and is priced on the probability that a certain type event, and hence amount of damage, will occur within a certain period.

This type of insurance reduces moral hazard, does not require individual evaluations, and can more easily be reinsured into international markets. Moreover, to further reduce transaction costs, insurance companies often do not distribute their products directly, but sell them through existing networks (such as those of MFIs).

In addition to the technical difficulties of developing an index, insurance companies in Bangladesh face two key legal and regulatory obstacles. First, the existing insurance law allows only licensed insurers to issue policies, and forbids institutions such as MFIs from acting as agents or brokers.[14] Second, under current legislation insurance companies must define insurable interests as under conventional property insurance, where losses are indemnified based on actual losses or damages to specified insured property. But with index insurance, there are no measures of actual losses—only the proxy payment triggered and measured by the index.

Notes

1. The government is supposed to repay half of the waived amounts, but that rarely happens.

2. For loans refinanced under the agriculture refinance facility, and before waivers, BKB and RAKUB have a spread of 3–4 percentage points.

3. Even under the more permissive provisioning rules for loans financed under the agriculture refinance facility, agricultural loans must be provisioned at 100 percent 60 months after their due date (Bangladesh Bank 2006b).

4. International experience shows that, if done properly, the risk of lending to micro, small, and medium-size enterprises is low, with a portfolio at risk above 30 days below 3 percent.

5. This section focuses on term loans because many MSMEs have no experience with bank borrowing. Thus term loans requiring frequent repayments are usually less risky and allow banks to test new clients. But provisioning is also lax for other types of loans (such as continuous loans).

6. While every bank chooses the organizational structure that suits it best, all successful lending programs for MSMEs have full-cycle loan officers. Personal relationships and knowledge are key for clients with a high degree of informality.

7. Although checks and balances must be in place and loan officers should not approve loans on their own, review by a central unit slows the growth of the loan portfolio. Most successful programs for lending to MSMEs use branch committees for loans under a certain amount—allowing for checks and balances while also ensuring speedy approval.

8. This report does not analyze the regime for immovable collateral because this complex topic requires separate analysis. As an indication of the complexity of the problem, an estimated 80 percent of cases pending in Bangladesh are related to land disputes.

9. Examples of competing creditors include tax authorities for tax arrears, lenders of overdue debts, suppliers of unpaid-for goods, receivers in bankruptcy, and judgment creditors to enforce court awards in their favor.

10. For example, financial leases on assets cannot be registered in this registry, and any liens on motor vehicles are registered in the motor vehicle registry.

11. Even with an upcoming computerization project supported by the Small Enterprise Development Facility, computer systems will be desktop- or network-based. Such systems require a lot of maintenance and training and are unsuitable for use by the general public.

12. For example, Arab Bangladesh Bank has one segment for all loans under 100 million taka; BASIC Bank has one segment for loans of 300,000–1,500,000 million taka; Dhaka Bank has one segment for loans of 300,000–5 million taka; Islamic Bank has two segments, one for loans of 200,000–5 million taka and one for loans of 5 million–10 million taka; and United Leasing Company has three segments, one for loans of less than 10 million taka, one for loans of 10 million–100 million taka, and one for loans of 100 million–300 million taka.

13. Although profitable guarantee levels for individual, multiperil crop insurance are related to a number of factors—including crop type, agro-ecological conditions, and the risk profile of a location—they usually do not exceed 65–75 percent.

14. The regulator seems to draw a distinction between potential index insurance products, which ideally should be reinsured, and microinsurance products issued by microfinance institutions (see chapter 1). The latter are allowed because the risks are retained by the microfinance institution, without the involvement of an insurance company. With index insurance the risks are transferred externally, because insurance companies transfer them to reinsurers.

CHAPTER 4

Increasing Access to Finance for the Missing Middle

This chapter offers suggestions on increasing access to finance for the rural missing middle. Government efforts should include improving the enabling environment and assisting institutions with the potential to expand access.

A number of policy options have the potential to increase access to finance for the missing middle. This chapter provides suggestions that are considered the most pragmatic in the current environment, that have proven successful in similar circumstances in other countries, and that could lead to relatively rapid, tangible improvements for the missing middle.

Given the historical significance of BKB and RAKUB, any effort to expand financial services in rural areas—especially for marginal, small, and medium size farmers—will necessarily involve these institutions. Their current market-distorting behavior only reinforces the importance of tackling their underlying problems. This chapter offers concrete suggestions for rehabilitating BKB and RAKUB and, for means of comparison, also estimates the costs of leaving them unreformed or closing them. This is not to say that increasing access to financial services for the missing middle could not also involve actions involving other institutions, such as cooperatives and BASIC. Exploring such options would be useful but would not detract from the need to tackle the challenges facing BKB and RAKUB.

In addition, steps could be taken to facilitate active participation by private banks and MFIs in increasing access to financial services for the missing middle. With the right enabling environment and appropriate lending methodologies, private banks could become major providers of loans to MSMEs—especially at the top end of the market. Unfortunately, given the current stage of development of the rural banking market, it seems unlikely that private banks will lend to MSMFs in the near future—especially if there continues to be no crop insurance system.

With suitable products and technology, MFIs could scale up their lending to MSMEs and MSMFs, especially to micro and small enterprises and marginal and small farmers. Given their experience and orientation, MFIs are likely to focus on the bottom end of these markets, at least in the medium term.

Finally, with the right enabling environment and development of the right products, insurance companies could begin to purchase at least part of the commercial agricultural risk pool, while commercially uninsurable risk could be covered by the government in a financially disciplined fashion. The following sections describe these recommendations in greater detail.

Transforming BKB and RAKUB into the Main Providers of Financial Services in Rural Areas

If rehabilitation of BKB and RAKUB is undertaken with the goal of restoring their long-term sustainability, it should focus on:

- Transforming the governance of the two banks, to protect them from political interference.
- Transferring the function of insurer of last resort for the agriculture sector to more appropriate institutions.
- Recapitalizing the banks in a way that frees them from the legacy of decades of losses—allowing them to make a fresh start.
- Restructuring operations so that the banks can provide cost-effective, well-designed financial services to rural markets.

Rehabilitating BKB and RAKUB would cost about 96 billion taka (see appendix 4). This undertaking would be a major challenge for the government and Bangladesh Bank—but if it succeeded, the two banks could significantly increase rural access to financial services. A few other countries, including Mongolia, have managed to reform agricultural banks (box 4.1).

Box 4.1

Khan Bank of Mongolia

Founded in 1991, the Agricultural Bank of Mongolia was designed to be the main provider of financial services in rural areas. But by 1999 the bank was in receivership due to many years of operating and credit losses. Management was poor, political interference was felt at every level of the bank, and it was failing to deliver financial services and products needed by rural communities.

In 2000 the bank was recapitalized and a new, donor-financed management team was installed. The bank's governance was reformed by creating an independent board of directors, with two members appointed by the donor, two members appointed by the government, and an independent chairperson.

The new management team focused on turning the Agricultural Bank into a full-service financial institution that could attract deposits and relend them in rural areas. The bank's staff was retrained, and in many cases underperforming managers and staff were replaced. Still, the number of staff members more than doubled as the bank opened new branches and offices in the countryside, with the number growing from 269 in 2000 to 379 in 2004. A key component of the bank's new strategy was to encourage growth in deposits by renewing lending (people tend to deposit where they can borrow, if needed). Many new lending products tailored to the needs of rural communities were introduced, as were other services (such as payments).

In late 2003 the Agricultural Bank of Mongolia was sold to a Japanese investment group and renamed Khan Bank. Between July 2000 and February 2004 the bank was transformed. During this period:

- Half of Mongolian households began using (and continue to use) Khan Bank.
- 900,000 new loans were made, averaging $382, with a default rate consistently below 2 percent.
- 90 percent of the bank's lending shifted to rural areas.
- Deposits grew 740 percent, while the share of government deposits in Khan Bank's total deposits fell from 50 percent to 7 percent.

Source: Dyer, Morrow, and Young 2004.

A comprehensive rehabilitation process for BKB and RAKUB would include:

- *Immediately placing the banks under tight supervisory controls to prevent them from incurring new losses, and installing independent temporary boards and competent temporary management.*[1] Although both banks are prime candidates for being placed under administration, doing so would likely be counterproductive as such announcements could trigger a run on deposits and, potentially, the collapse of both banks. It might be more practical to place both banks under tight supervisory control using consensual arrangements—possibly in the form of supervisory agreements—and, given the banks' state ownership, the government could compel them to cooperate. A team of senior supervisors would be placed in each bank to monitor its activities and all management decisions would be subject to confirmation by the supervisors. The banks would not be allowed to take further deposits until after recapitalization and a new management structure were in place. Tight liquidity controls would be placed on branches and loans, and expenditures would also become subject to approval by the supervisory teams. If the government wants to continue lending to farmers during this period, and in order to explore new lending methodologies, special offices could be created to pilot new agricultural products. These pilots would ensure that farmers continue to receive credit and that new lending methodologies are trialed, so that once the banks are in a position to start lending again, the pilots could be rolled out to other branches.

- *Updating financial data and conducting diagnostics for both banks.* Audits—using international financial reporting standards—should be conducted to determine the up-to-date costs of rehabilitating the two banks. Diagnosing each bank's systems and governance would generate detailed recommendations for new systems and governance as well as opportunities for reducing operating costs, primarily (though not exclusively) from automation.

- *Deciding whether to merge the two banks.* Given the potential efficiencies of a merger, and the fact that the combined bank could use a single information technology package to support new systems and controls, there seems to be a strong argument in favor of merging BKB and RAKUB during the rehabilitation process. Moreover, rehabilitating a merged bank would simplify the technical assistance required and reduce the management challenges involved.

- *Preparing a detailed recapitalization plan.* Using information from the financial diagnostic, this plan would model the restructuring of each bank (or the merged bank) and determine the financial instruments and amounts required to restore them to full compliance with regulatory capital requirements, prudent liquidity levels (cash and cash equivalents equal to about 20 percent of deposits), and at least zero pretax net income and positive operating cash flows. The design of recapitalization instruments would also have to reduce and restructure the terms of the banks' borrowing from Bangladesh Bank to sustainable levels. The recapitalization would mostly be in the form of bonds to provide the banks with liquidity only to the extent that they become able to redeploy it prudently, by complying with detailed financial and operational indicators, and to reduce the immediate fiscal impact. As part of the recapitalization plan, a decision would need to be made on whether to invite development-oriented investors (such as the International Finance Corporation, Asian Development Bank, Agha Khan Foundation, or Japan Bank for International Cooperation) to make minority investments in BKB and RAKUB. The goals of such investment would be to reduce the short-term cost of recapitalization and improve the banks' long-term governance and operations (box 4.2). In many countries development-oriented investors interested in holding minority shares have made meaningful contributions by lowering recapitalization costs, strengthening governance, reducing political interference and ensuring sustainability in financial institutions with a developmental mandate.

- *Developing a new business strategy and business plan to allow the banks to operate prudently and profitably and to serve rural markets.* Experiences in Mongolia, Tanzania, and Thailand indicate that rural-focused banks with suitable governance and investors with the standing to resist political pressure can function prudently while serving a broader social mission. To ensure that the banks maintain their focus on rural areas and on agriculture, their activities in large cities could be limited and the banks could be required to lend a certain percentage of the loan portfolio to the agricultural sector. As part of their new business models, BKB and RAKUB's current quasi-insurance functions should be excluded from their mandates, as the banks lack the technical, operational, and financial capacity required to provide insurance services. While it is legitimate for the government to protect farmers against the financial consequences of natural disasters, this function should be provided by specialized entities, such as insurance companies (see below, in the section on weather risk management).
- *Creating a bank rehabilitation unit.* Such a unit, in the Ministry of Finance or at Bangladesh Bank would oversee and control the banks' activities during the rehabilitation process.

Box 4.2

Benefits of Having Development-Oriented Investors as Minority Shareholders

Inviting development-oriented investors to be minority shareholders can bring two major benefits: lowering recapitalization costs and improving governance and operations.

Lowering recapitalization costs. Development-oriented investors can make a significant contribution to the capital of the bank concerned. Although they would not help cover historical losses (which should be covered by the government during the restructuring process), they would invest in the new capital structure of the bank—giving it additional financial strength and better enabling it to fulfill its development function. In addition, development investors may be willing to provide additional financial resources (such as by extending credit lines to the bank or financing technical assistance for operational restructuring) alongside their capital investment to provide liquidity so that the restructured bank can build its new business.

Improving governance and operations. To invite development-oriented minority shareholders, the government would develop and commit to:

- A detailed business plan for the restructured bank. Once the plan has been agreed to, it becomes a legally binding document.
- Appointing a board of directors composed mainly of independent professionals. This arrangement is designed to increase the board's competence and independence, and in turn improve the quality of its management supervision and ability to exercise independent governance.
- Having large credit decisions and changes in credit policies unanimously approved by the board. This approach provides further insulation from political interference in the bank's decision making.

Rehabilitating BKB and RAKUB would likely take up to three years. The rehabilitation period is long for two reasons. First, it would take time to implement comprehensive operational and system improvements. The banks require a complete overhaul, and modernization of their information technology and staff—from tellers in branches to senior management— would require extensive training in how to use the new systems. Second, the banks require an overhaul of their business strategies, involving the development and implementation of new policies and procedures for all aspects of bank operations and the development and introduction of new credit, deposit, and service products, all requiring extensive training of staff and management and the introduction of new technology. There are two alternatives to rehabilitating BKB and RAKUB: doing nothing or closing the two banks (box 4.3).

Box 4.3

Financial Costs of Alternatives to Rehabilitating BKB and RAKUB

The government has three policy options for addressing BKB and RAKUB's insolvencies. The first is a "do nothing" strategy that would leave the banks unreformed. The second is to close and liquidate the banks. The third is to rehabilitate them. The costs of rehabilitation are estimated at 96 billion taka; the costs of the first two options are estimated below.

Doing nothing

The government could simply do nothing to address the problems posed by BKB and RAKUB. Under this option the two banks would remain open but unreformed, and Bangladesh Bank or the Ministry of Finance would need to keep advancing additional funds to pay the banks' operating expenses and keep some credit flowing to their customers. This approach might be feasible for up to three years—but at that point accumulated operating losses would be so high that the banks would have to be liquidated or recapitalized.

Assuming that no less than 10 billion taka a year in new funds were provided to BKB and RAKUB by Bangladesh Bank or the Ministry of Finance, the banks would incur additional credit losses of 7–8 billion taka a year (see the table). This estimate, based on the banks' track records, assumes that for every taka of additional financing provided to the banks, 70–80 percent would turn into nonperforming loans.

Closing and liquidating BKB and RAKUB

In addition to the social and economic costs, closing and liquidating RKB and RAKUB would have a high one-time fiscal cost. These costs are driven by the banks' state ownership and their extensive entanglement with the state on both the asset and liability sides of their balance sheets. State ownership means that there is an implicit guarantee of the banks' deposits, so these would have to be paid off

(Continued)

in full and in cash. The banks' second largest source of liabilities, Bangladesh Bank, has a government guarantee of its lending to the two banks and would be bankrupted if the government did not pay these guarantees. Finally, the banks' employees are civil servants, and so are entitled to compensation and pension benefits for which the government is responsible. It is difficult to quantify this liability, but it would be substantial given the size of the banks' workforces and payrolls. Liquidating the banks would cost more than 100 billion taka, excluding the staff compensation and pension benefits.

Government Costs of Options for Resolving BKB and RAKUB
(millions of taka, based on 30 June, 2005, balance sheets)

	Cost				Overall
Option	Year 1	Year 2	Year 3	Total	Total
Doing nothing but					
provide refinancing	13.5	13.5	13.5	40.5	141.5
Operating losses	6.0	6.0	6.0	18.0	18.0
Losses from new lending	7.5	7.5	7.5	22.5	22.5
Liquidation costs					101.0
Closing and liquidating	129.0	−14.0	−14.0	101.0	101.0
Paying off liabilities	143.0			143.0	143.0
Recoveries from assets	−14.0	−14.0	−14.0	−42.0	−42.0

Source: Authors' calculations based on BKB and RAKUB audited financial statements 2005.

Helping Banks Serve Rural MSMEs

To facilitate bank lending to MSMEs, the government could promote an enabling environment that makes such lending less costly. The government could also support grant-funded technical assistance to help some banks adapt their lending procedures to significantly increase such lending.[2]

Improving the enabling environment

To reduce the costs of serving MSMEs, Bangladesh Bank could reduce provisioning requirements on such loans to 1 percent—the same share it requires for consumer loans and loans issued under the refinance facility for small and medium-size enterprises. Bangladesh Bank could also allow movable collateral not in the possession of banks among assets whose value can be discounted when calculating provisions. In parallel, the government could reform the legal framework for secured transactions and upgrade the registry to enable all businesses to safely register pledges on movable assets.

Bangladesh's credit bureau should be strengthened to reduce information asymmetries between lenders and borrowers. Bangladesh Bank could upgrade the services provided by the bureau by:

- Ensuring that the bureau's data are electronically accessible by financial institutions, as this will shorten delivery times for credit reports and ensure that the bureau's information is up to date.
- Requiring that banks provide reports in real time on all loans above 50,000 taka.
- Increasing the amount of information in the credit bureau, including guarantees provided by borrowers, other information on outstanding loans, and a list of other businesses of borrowers.

Strengthening lending technology

Technical assistance to improve lending technology should focus on the key obstacles to increasing lending to the missing middle (see chapter 3). Because not every bank will be a suitable candidate for lending to MSMEs, technical assistance should be given only to those fully committed to it. Serving such enterprises profitably requires more than just introducing new products and procedures: it also requires changing the entire corporate culture and the way that banks operate. Hence technical assistance should go only to banks whose investors' mandates mesh with these changes. Banks with large branch networks and a focus on retail lending usually have a comparative advantage in entering this market segment, but smaller private banks could also be targeted to serve as catalysts.

Although many countries have developed lending programs for MSMEs in state-owned banks with large networks, success usually takes a few years because the banks are often slow in implementing the required changes. This is why technical assistance should also be given to a few other banks—including smaller, faster-moving private banks. But while such banks are faster in implementing changes at the beginning, acting as a catalyst for the state-owned banks, they reach a plateau after a few years due to their smaller networks. Like Khan Bank in Mongolia, reformed BKB and RAKUB could be suitable candidates for technical assistance to state banks.

The assistance program should be comprehensive and cover the entire loan cycle. It should last at least two years and involve resident advisors.

And it should include a redesign of bank products to meet client needs, a robust management information system, and a scheme to ensure that staff incentives are aligned with banks' efficiency targets.

Finally, the technical assistance program should include performance agreements setting minimum targets, signed by the partner bank and the technical assistance provider (and its funder, if different). These agreements should specify the number and volume of loans disbursed and outstanding to be achieved by a given date, as well as an indicator of portfolio quality (such as keeping the portfolio at risk over 30 days to less than 3 percent). These targets should be monitored monthly, and remedial actions should be taken if they are not met.

Helping Microfinance Institutions Scale Up Lending to the Missing Middle

Meeting the needs of MSMEs and MSMFs requires that MFIs transform their operations and themselves—from social mobilizers to commercial providers of financial services. Changes are needed in their staff training, lending methodologies, and use of management information systems. The challenge will obviously be greater for smaller MFIs, but even larger ones will have to make major adjustments.

Like banks, it is easier for MFIs to serve MSMEs than MSMFs. Private banks are unlikely to serve these farmers in the near future. So, whether BKB and RAKUB are left to languish or are restructured, MFIs will need to step up lending to this segment. A few MFIs, such as Banco Procredit, have managed to lend profitably to MSMFs (box 4.4). To help the microfinance industry make this shift, the government could promote a technical assistance fund to help selected institutions upgrade their lending methods and management information systems, and even use technology to cut the cost of serving remote areas (box 4.5).

Promoting Weather Risk Management for MSMFs

To help banks and MFIs lend to MSMFs, the government could promote—and in some cases, sponsor—risk transfer mechanisms. To ensure that private insurance companies are not crowded out, the risk should be segmented, and insurance products that are commercially viable should be sold by the private sector. Insurance products that are not viable, either because they are too expensive or because they cover events that, though very destructive, occur very rarely, can instead be covered through direct government intervention.

Box 4.4

Banco Procredit's Expansion into Rural Areas

Like many Bangladeshi microfinance institutions, El Salvador's Calpia began as an urban nongovernmental organization in 1988 to provide emergency relief after a natural disaster caused by an earthquake. It transformed into a formal regulated finance company in 1995 and into a bank in 2004, when it was renamed Banco Procredit El Salvador.

A pilot agricultural product was tested successfully in 1993–95, and a refined version of the product was mainstreamed in Calpia's activities. The product's design includes the following elements:

- *Interview, application, and verification.* Loan officers interview potential clients, asking about farming or nonagricultural economic activities, sources of income for repayment, purpose of the loan, sources of collateral, and credit history. Officers also visit potential clients' home or place of business (sometimes both) to view household relationships, potential collateral, and documentation (such as receipts for purchases and sales and titles for property).
- *Credit report.* Loan officers evaluate the information obtained and use computers to prepare appraisal reports. A cash-flow projection is prepared based on the expected quantity and timing of household revenues and expenses. A balance sheet is also prepared, listing household, farm, and business assets, their values, and outstanding liabilities. Collateral is identified and valued, and the capacity to pay of any proposed co-signers is evaluated.
- *Credit committee.* The credit committee approves, modifies, or rejects loan applications presented by loan officers. The process is rapid for loans under about $15,000, with the decision often made the day the report is submitted. Larger loans take longer because they must be reviewed in the head office.
- *Loan terms and conditions.* Agricultural loans are made for an average of 10 months and livestock loans for 15–18 months. Some interest and partial principal payments are requested from clients projected to have the necessary cash flow. Otherwise a single payment is required at loan maturity, for both interest and principal. Annual nominal interest rates are 27 percent, charged on unpaid principal. A 4 percent origination fee is charged for single payment loans, and 2 percent for loans with multiple payments.

(Continued)

- *Disbursement, monitoring, and contract enforcement:* To minimize fraud, loans are usually disbursed as lump sums in a branch office, and all payments must be made there. Penalty interest of up to 5 percent of the loan balance may be assessed for late payments. A late payment agreement can be arranged if the delay is expected to be temporary, but collateral may be seized if late payment persists for 30 days.

With almost 140,000 depositors, more than 70,000 borrowers, and profitable operations since the early 1990s, Banco Procredit is one of Latin America's largest microfinance institutions. Moreover, its rural portfolio grew from 18 percent of its total portfolio in 1996 to 32 percent in 2006.

Source: Gonzalez-Vega, Rodriguez-Meza, and Pleitez-Chaves 2002; Navajas and Gonzalez-Vega 2003; Buchenau and Meyer 2007.

The government could launch two initiatives to this end. First, it could promote the development of a pilot commercial index insurance product by:

- Removing legal and regulatory restrictions on agents distributing insurance policies and allowing the proxy payment triggered to be considered the actual loss (see chapter 3).
- Promoting the creation of a technical assistance unit that helps interested institutions develop the technical side of the product and encourages interested participants (insurance companies and MFIs) to participate in the pilot phase. Because insurance companies might be reluctant to enter this market segment individually, an organizational arrangement could be developed between insurers and reinsurers.[3] Initially a drought insurance product, similar to that developed in India by BASIX-ICICI (box 4.6), could be piloted. If successful, it could be followed by a flood index product requiring more detailed feasibility analysis.

Second, given the weakness of the insurance sector, the government could create a Fund for Natural Calamities to cover adverse weather events such as floods. To avoid excessive fiscal exposure to adverse natural events, a contingent debt facility could be created to cover any contingent payments required should floods occur.[4] The fund would, in a sense, substitute

Box 4.5

Using Technology to Improve Financial Access in Uganda

Three Ugandan microfinance institutions—Uganda Microfinance Union, FINCA UGANDA, and FOCCAS Uganda—have introduced a remote transaction system to provide more convenient services to their clients, reduce costs for their clients and themselves, and strengthen their management information systems.

The remote transaction system hardware consists of a battery-powered point of sale device with an interface, smart card reader, numeric keypad, and printer. Using cell phone infrastructure, the system can convey data to a transaction server connected to each microfinance institution's back office. Staff members then use a Web-based server to view transaction histories and manage client accounts.

The three institutions take different approaches in using the remote transaction system to reach clients. FOCCAS's loan officers take the point of sale terminal to group meetings, where they conduct loan payments, savings, and other financial transactions related to the group fund. FINCA UGANDA piloted the system in one of its sub-branches. FINCA tellers travel to collect money from group leaders at the sub-branch twice a week and use the terminal to capture group information electronically. The cash is then deposited in the nearest commercial bank. Finally, the Uganda Microfinance Union has third-party agents (local merchants) using the system to provide financial services to its clients. As cash transactions are carried out between clients and agents, electronic cash transactions are executed at the institution. Client and agent accounts are then debited or credited as applicable. At the end of each day, all the transactions on the point of sale terminal are uploaded on the remote transaction system.

Source: Firpo 2005; Hewlett-Packard 2005.

for BKB and RAKUB's role of insurers of last resort. It would also provide needed technical, operational, and financial discipline in the financing of natural disasters. The fund should comply with basic insurance principles, including disbursement rules that allow farmers affected by natural disasters to get immediate payouts. The payments would be triggered by an objective and transparent index (for example, using remote sensing technology), and farmers could use them to repay loans.

As a risk financing mechanism, the Fund for Natural Calamities would not be effective at covering recurrent losses generated, for example, by

Box 4.6

BASIX and ICICI's Drought Index Insurance Product

BASIX is an Indian MFI, based in Andhra Pradesh, with operations in more than 10,000 villages and about 200,000 customers. In 2003, in collaboration with the ICICI Lombard General Insurance Company, BASIX designed a rainfall-indexed insurance product. The pilot pursued a business model in which the insurance company, along with a reinsurance arrangement, takes on all the risk (see figure). BASIX simply acts an intermediary that receives commissions by selling the product to its customers. BASIX and the insurance company both incur administrative expenses from the operation.

Structure of the Product

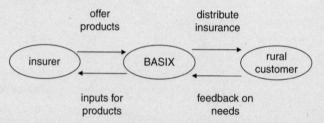

During the 2003 pilot the insurance contracts were designed to protect farmers from drought during the groundnut and castor growing season. ICICI Lombard underwrote the products, which BASIX extension officers marketed and sold in four villages. In total, 230 farmers bought the insurance for the Kharif monsoon season (June–September)—and most were small farmers, with less than 2.5 acres of land. ICICI Lombard reinsured the risk using a major reinsurance company.

In 2004 the program was significantly modified in terms of geography, product design, and scope. To minimize basis risk (the mismatch between insurance payouts and crop losses), the product included a three-phase payout structure that reflects the weighted importance of rainfall during crop sowing, growth, and harvest. In 2005 BASIX and ICICI Lombard further improved the product by adding features (such as a varying starting date) recommended by farmers. In addition, instead of crop-specific policies, BASIX sells area-specific generic weather insurance products that suit all major rainfed crops in the same agro-climatic region.

(Continued)

Between June 2003 and March 2006 BASIX sold 7,653 rainfall insurance policies in six Indian states. For the first two years it did not make profits, but since the program was scaled up in 2005, BASIX has earned about 350,000 rupees from its commission fee (equal to 15 percent of collected premiums). Total administrative expenses account for 22 percent of premiums, which is comparable to that for other insurance products. The product developed by BASIX and ICICI has been scaled up by other insurance companies—mainly AICI, which in 2006 sold more than 250,000 such policies.

Source: Manuamorn 2005.

Box 4.7

Mexico's Fund for Natural Disasters

In 1996 Mexico created a Fund for Natural Disasters (FONDEN) as a last resort source of financing to rebuild public infrastructure and compensate low-income producers for crop and livestock losses after natural disasters. The fund is a disaster relief program rather than an insurance program, but the agricultural component has characteristics similar to crop insurance programs—for example, loss claims trigger field inspections. Farmers' claims are settled at a predetermined level per hectare, and assistance is capped at 5 hectares per farmer, which is both efficient and weights the assistance to smaller holders. Irrigated or insured land is ineligible.

The fund was initially financed through annual budget allocations, exposing it to fiscal uncertainties. This fund's reliance on budget contribution was reduced in 2007 with the introduction of a commercial risk transfer strategy, including the purchase of reinsurance and the issuance of a catastrophe bond. This market-based strategy ensures that FONDEN can access up to $450 million if a major earthquake hits Mexico City.

nonviable farming practices. Hence mitigation projects and projects should be developed to promote viable farming practices, and the implementing agencies should work closely with the fund.

The Fund for Natural Calamities would not exclude the commercial insurance industry. On the contrary, it would develop new risk transfer products and pass them to the insurance industry once they became commercially viable. Thus the fund would fill the gap between farmers' needs for protection against natural disasters and the lack of agriculture insurance. Accordingly, the fund should focus on experimental business activities, while viable agricultural insurance activities would be left to commercial insurance companies. Such a public-private partnership in the financing of natural calamities has been implemented in several countries, including Mexico (box 4.7).

Notes

1. Both banks have signed memorandums of understanding with Bangladesh Bank that include, among other things, capping loan portfolio growth at 5 percent a year. But neither bank is in compliance with these agreements.

2. A number of countries, including China and several in Eastern Europe and the Commonwealth of Independent States, have adopted similar schemes for both state and private banks—generally with very successful results.

3. A successful pool of insurance companies was developed in Mongolia, where index livestock insurance has been developed.

4. Mongolia recently established a similar facility to support its index-based livestock insurance scheme.

Definitions Used in this Report

Rural Areas

Because the ultimate goal of this report is to formulate a realistic strategy for sustainably increasing rural access to financial services and because, as of 2005, 72 percent of lending (by volume) occurred in the cities of Dhaka and Chittagong, the report uses a broader definition of rural than is normally used in Bangladesh. Here rural lending refers to all intermediation activity that happens outside those two cities. Like everywhere, in Bangladesh financial institutions operating profitably gradually enter more difficult market segments, as competition intensifies in segments where they are already active. Hence it is not realistic to expect financial institutions to jump from operating mainly in Dhaka and Chittagong to operating in rural villages.

Micro, Small, and Medium-Size Enterprises

There are two official definitions of small and medium-size enterprises, one used by Bangladesh Bank and the other by the Ministry of Industry. Both use economic sector as the main criterion for grouping these enterprises: Bangladesh Bank's definition differentiates between three sectors (services, trading, manufacturing), while the Ministry of Industry uses only two (manufacturing and nonmanufacturing). Both definitions use asset and employment criteria to further classify these enterprises (tables A1.1 and A1.2).

When considered from a perspective of increasing access to financial services, both of these definitions present problems. First, both were created to classify small and medium-size enterprises as one group within the national economy, divided primarily by sector rather than size. Thus the definitions are of limited value for service providers—such as banks—seeking to understand and cater to the needs of specific segments of small and medium-size enterprises.

Second, the two official definitions are very broad. For example, almost all small and medium-size enterprises employ far fewer employees than the maximum thresholds set by the definitions.[1] Similarly, smaller enterprises in these sectors average much lower asset values than those stipulated by the definitions.

A definition that is useful for financial institutions should describe a unique target market and its specific demands. In Bangladesh, as elsewhere, loan size is the most important factor considered by financial institutions when designing new products. Hence this report defines small and medium-size enterprises based on their capacity to absorb credit. Because a business's ability to absorb credit is closely related to its

Table A1.1. Definition of Small and Medium-Size Enterprises Used by Bangladesh Bank, by Sector

Economic sector	Total asset value excluding land and buildings (taka)	Maximum number of employees
Service	50,000–3,000,000	30
Trading	3,000,000–5,000,000	20
Manufacturing	5,000,000–10,000,000	60

Source: Bangladesh Bank data.

Table A1.2. Definition of Small and Medium-Size Enterprises Used by the Ministry of Industry, by Sector

Economic sector	Category	Total asset value excluding land and buildings (taka)	Maximum number of employees
Manufacturing	Small	<15,000,000	n.a.
	Medium-size	15,000,000–100,000,000	n.a.
Nonmanufacturing	Small	n.a.	<25
	Medium-size	n.a.	25–100

Source: Ministry of Industry data.
Note: n.a. = not applicable.

Table A1.3. Definition of MSMEs Used in This Report
(*taka*)

Segment	Credit absorption capacity	Annual profit
Micro	50,000–300,000	50,000–170,000
Small	300,001–1,000,000	170,001–540,000
Medium-size	1,000,001–3,000,000	540,001–5,000,000

Source: Authors.
Note: The credit limit for medium-size enterprises can potentially increase to 5,000,000 taka as institutions gain experience with lending.

profitability, here the latter is used as a proxy for credit absorption capacity. Moreover, to allow for homogeneous market segments, and given the different nature of the bottom and top ends of this sector, this definition is further divided into micro, small, and medium-size enterprises (table A1.3).[2] The floor for the microenterprise definition is set at a loan size of 50,000 taka, as supply-side data show that microfinance institutions provide good coverage below that level.

Marginal, Small, and Medium-Size Farmers

Marginal, small, and medium-size farmers are defined using the definition from the Bangladesh Agricultural Census: marginal farmers are those with landholdings of 0.5–1.49 acres, small farmers those with 1.5–2.49 acres, and medium-size those with 2.5–7.5 acres. In terms of loan size, although the amount to be borrowed by acre depends on the level of mechanization, type of crop, and other factors, 9,000 taka an acre (which is what PKSF partner organizations offer under the recently created farmers lending program) is a realistic estimate. Based on this estimate, average loans to this market segment would range from 4,500–67,500 taka.

Notes

1. The average MSME has 4.3 employees according to Daniels (2003), or 4.4 employees according to the 2006 Rural MSME Finance Survey.

2. For example, microenterprises are highly sensitive to loan processing time and collateral requirements, and less sensitive to interest rate costs. Microenterprises also often have low levels of formality—for example, they rarely have written financial statements.

Comparing Rural Lending in Bangladesh and India

This appendix compares rural lending patterns in Bangladesh and India. Data for Bangladesh refer to financial activities outside the cities of Dhaka and Chittagong, which include cities with up to 700,000 people, while data for India refer to rural and semiurban areas based on the Reserve Bank of India's definition—that is, towns with fewer than 100,000 inhabitants. Thus the data for India paint a conservative picture of the country's financial intermediation in rural areas.

Given this, the rural-urban divide in bank lending is likely to be bigger in Bangladesh than in India. In 2005 the difference between loan-deposit ratios in rural and urban India was 26 percentage points, while in Bangladesh it was 37 percentage points (figure A2.1). In India rural lending accounted for 21 percent of bank loans, compared with 27 percent in Bangladesh (figure A2.2). And between 1996 and 2005 agricultural bank lending fell by 7 percentage points in Bangladesh, while in India it remained stable—and in 2005 increased by 1 percentage point over 2004 (figure A2.3).

Banks are the largest providers of rural loans in both countries, accounting for 72 percent in Bangladesh and 61 percent in India (figure A2.4). In India cooperatives are the second largest provider of rural loans (38 percent), while in Bangladesh MFIs are (20 percent)—and cooperatives account for just 4 percent of the total.

Figure A2.1. Proportion of Loans to Deposits by Bank Branch Location, 1996–2005
(percent)

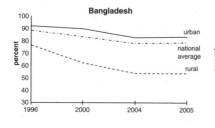

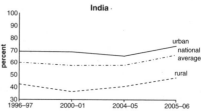

Source: Bangladesh Bank data.   *Source:* Reserve Bank of India data.

Figure A2.2. Urban and Rural Shares of Bank Loans

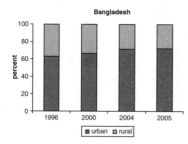

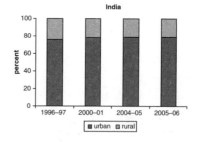

Source: Bangladesh Bank data.   *Source:* Reserve Bank of India data and World Bank 2006a.

Figure A2.3. Distribution of Bank Loans, by Purpose

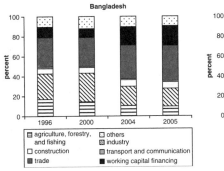

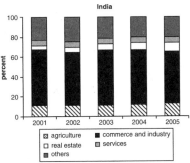

Source: Bangladesh Bank data.

Source: Reserve Bank of India data and World Bank 2006a.

Figure A2.4. Estimated Rural Lending by Source, 2005

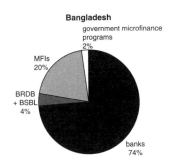

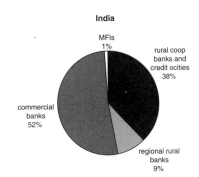

Source: Authors' calculations based on Bangladesh Bank and PKSF data.

Source: Authors' calculations based on World Bank 2006a and Sa-Dhan 2006.

The Rural Micro, Small, and Medium-Size Enterprise Finance Survey

In April and May 2006 the World Bank, Business and Finance Consulting (BFC), in cooperation with HB Consultants, surveyed 226 MSMEs in the Rajshahi and Moulvibazar districts on their demand for financial services. Respondents were evenly divided between the two districts. The survey used a multistage sampling technique.

Survey Questionnaire

The survey had three sections. The first gathered basic information, such as district and location of business, and gender of the respondent.

The second section collected demographic information such as age and education of the respondent, as well as data on the enterprise's primary economic sector of activity, number of employees, and ownership structure and legal status. Information was also collected on the revenues and cost structures of the enterprises surveyed.

The third section compiled information on use of and access to financial services such as savings, loans, and remittances. Questions were asked on whether the respondent saves; if so, whether he or she saves in a financial institution; and, where applicable, the barriers to saving. On the use of payment services, questions were asked about the frequency of use, average amount exchanged, travel time required to visit the institution if financial institutions were used, and so on. Respondents were then asked whether they had sought a loan in the three years prior to the survey and, where applicable, reasons for not applying to formal sources. Those who had received loans (whether from formal or informal sources) were asked to provide details on the terms and conditions of their loan contracts. Finally, respondents were asked to estimate the amount of external financing they will need in 2006, which external financing sources they would seek, and their preferred terms and conditions for loan sizes, terms, and interest rates.

Sampling Frame

The sampling frame was based on a list compiled using data from chambers of commerce and local authorities. The list included 199,552 enterprises in the Rajshahi district and 148,970 in the Moulvibazar district. These districts were chosen for two reasons. First, agribusiness is important in both (agribusiness being one of the sectors with the biggest growth potential in rural Bangladesh). Second, the team conducted case studies on bank branches in the districts, allowing for cross-checking of information (such as the estimated time required to get a loan from a bank).

Sample Selection

The survey used a multistage sampling technique.

- The first stratum coincided with district; 150 enterprises were surveyed in each of the two districts selected for the study (Rajshahi and Moulvibazar).
- The second stratum was defined by three locations of enterprises: urban, semi-urban, and rural. To ensure a sufficient number of responses from each group, 25 percent, 50 percent, and 25 percent of respondents came from each respective category. The urban, semi-urban, and rural locations were chosen using a cluster analysis weighted by population within each district.
- The third stratum was the economic sector. In rural areas all selected enterprises were agricultural enterprises. Elsewhere, enterprises were divided into three sectors, with the number of respondents from each sector proportional to the sector's share of production for micro, small, and medium-size enterprises as a whole—50 percent trade, 24 percent

services and 26 percent manufacturing. Within each district and economic sector surveyed, enterprises were selected randomly using lists developed by HB Consultants, based on information provided by chambers of commerce and local authorities.

Map A3.1. Bangladesh, with Survey Areas Highlighted

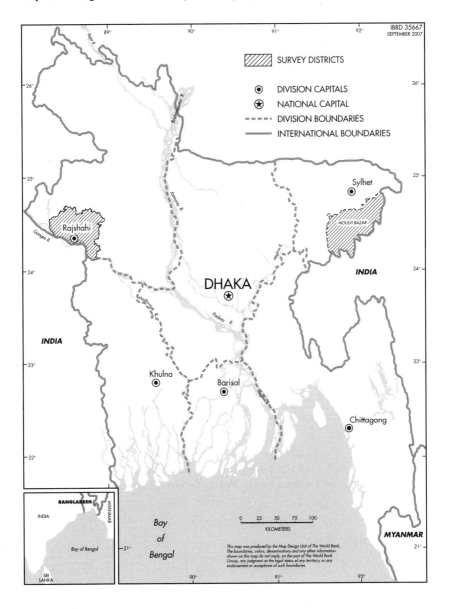

Focus Group Discussions

In addition to the survey, BFC and the World Bank organized four focus group discussions, each with 7–10 participants. Two discussions were conducted prior to the survey, and two afterward. Discussion group participants were selected using information provided by chambers of commerce, banks, and local authorities.

Basic Sample Data

The tables below report the sample composition by sector, number of employees by enterprise size, legal status and location of enterprises, and years of schooling of enterprise owners. The average enterprise had been in operation for 11.6 years.

Table A3.1. Sectoral Distribution of Sampled Enterprises

Sector/subsector	Number	Share of total (percent)
Trade	**114**	**50.4**
Wholesale	36	15.9
Retail	78	34.5
Services	**54**	**23.9**
Hotels, restaurants, catering	19	8.4
Transportation	19	8.4
Other	16	7.1
Manufacturing	**58**	**25.7**
Textiles and apparel	5	2.2
Wood and furniture	18	8.0
Food and beverages	11	4.9
Light engineering	17	7.5
Leather goods	4	1.8
Other	3	1.3
Total	**226**	**100.0**

Source: Rural MSME Finance Survey 2006.

Table A3.2. Average Number of Employees of Sampled Enterprises, by Enterprise Size

Size	Number
Micro	4
Small	8
Medium-size	10

Source: Rural MSME Finance Survey 2006.

Table A3.3. Legal Status of Sampled Enterprises

Status	Number of enterprises	Share of total (percent)
Not registered with authorities	3	1.3
Privately held limited company	1	0.4
Sole proprietorship	218	96.5
Partnership	4	1.8
Total	226	100.0

Source: Rural MSME Finance Survey 2006.

Table A3.4. Location of Business of Sampled Enterprises

Location	Number of enterprises	Share of total (percent)
Dedicated premises	60	26.5
Home	7	3.1
Marketplace	112	49.5
In the street	47	20.8
Total	226	100.0

Source: Rural MSME Finance Survey 2006.

Table A3.5. Average Years of Schooling for Owners of Sampled Enterprises

Number of years	Number of enterprises	Share of total (percent)
None	4	1.8
1–5	32	14.2
6–10	100	44.2
11–12	44	19.5
13 or more	46	20.3
Total	226	100.0

Source: Rural MSME Finance Survey 2006.

Recapitalization Scenarios and Costs of Closing BKB and RAKUB

Costs of Recapitalizing BKB

Efforts to recapitalize BKB should aim to restore the bank to complete financial health. Tables A4.1 and A4.2 provide two scenarios for the recapitalization of BKB. The first is a realistic scenario where, based on a diagnostic audit,[1] 50 percent of loans graded standard in June 2005 are found to be classifiable. The second is an optimistic scenario where only 25 percent of standard loans are found to be classifiable after a diagnostic audit. In both scenarios the entire portfolio of the bank's substandard or worse loans (after classification by a diagnostic audit) are carved out of the bank, leaving it with a fully performing (payments of principal and interest made on time) loan portfolio. Other items are also carved out:

- BKB's claims on the government that have not been met (1,716 million taka) are booked as investments.
- A wide variety of assets representing claims for remission of interest, principal waivers, capitalized losses, and miscellaneous items that appear to be of no value (15,590 million taka) are booked as other assets.
- BKB borrowing from Bangladesh Bank (33,389 million taka).
- BKB borrowing directly from the government (148 million taka).

The difference between the book value of the assets removed and the value of liabilities transferred results in a reduction of the bank's capital of 29,399 million taka in the realistic scenario and 19,178 taka in the optimistic scenario (with the difference between the two outcomes being caused by the reduced quantity of standard loans removed in the optimistic scenario).

After carving out bad assets and offsetting some of the cost to the bank of doing so by removing liabilities, BKB's capital would be extremely negative. To restore it to financial health, the bank would then be recapitalized to about a 12 percent capital adequacy ratio with an injection of 47,983 million taka in government bonds in the realistic scenario and 38,988 million taka in the optimistic scenario. These calculations use a 12 percent capital adequacy ratio rather than the regulatory minimum of 9 percent to allow for the absorption of continued operating losses while BKB is restructured and to provide some scope for renewed lending, which would increase BKB's risk assets. The exact amount of capital needed would be determined only after diagnostic work has been completed and a business plan prepared, but would not be less than the amounts shown in tables A4.1 and A4.2.

Table A4.1. BKB Recapitalization: Realistic Scenario with 50 Percent of Standard Loans Carved Out

(based on 30 June 2005 balance sheet; millions of taka)

Item	Audited	Carve out bad assets	Adjusted	Recapitalize to 12% capital adequacy ratio	Recapitalized
Total liquid assets	6,802	0	6,802	0	6,802
Cash on hand	4,024		4,024		4,024
Deposits with other banks	2,778		2,778		2,778
Investments (1)	1,719	−1,716	3	47,983	47,986
Net loans and advances	65,673	−45,231	20,443	0	20,443
Standard	40,885	−20,443	20,443		20,443
Substandard	4,763	−4,763	0		0
Doubtful	4,738	−4,738	0		0
Loss	15,287	−15,287	0		0
Fixed assets	935		935		935
Other assets (2)	20,154	−15,990	4,164		4,164
Total assets (3)	**95,283**	**−62,936**	**32,347**	**47,983**	**80,330**

Table A4.1. BKB Recapitalization: Realistic Scenario with 50 Percent of Standard Loans Carved Out *(continued)*
(based on 30 June 2005 balance sheet; millions of taka)

Item	Audited	Carve out bad assets	Adjusted	Recapitalize to 12% capital adequacy ratio	Recapitalized
Total borrowings	34,243	−33,537	706	0	706
Borrowing from Bangladesh Bank	33,389	−33,389	0		0
Borrowing from government	148	−148	0		0
Borrowing from other banks	706		706		706
Deposits and bills payable	56,345		56,345		56,345
Other liabilities	20,216		20,216		20,216
Total liabilities	**110,804**	**−33,537**	**77,267**	**0**	**77,267**
Paid-up capital	2,400		2,400		2,400
Statutory reserves	0		0		0
Other reserves	1,305		1,305		1,305
Retained earnings	−19,224	−29,399	−48,623	47,983	−640
Total capital	**−15,519**	**−29,399**	**−44,918**	**47,983**	**3,065**
Total liabilities and capital (3)	**−95,285**	**−62,936**	**32,349**	**47,983**	**80,332**

Notes:

(1) Investments

Government bond	1,715,879,478

(2) Other assets suspense adjustment for remission of interest

Receivable from government	5,785,705,527
Interest on flood affected loans	20,426,576
Interest on frozen tea loan	5,322,078
Pre-liberation loans interest	39,962,414
Weavers credit	60,621,926
Transferable remission of interest	320,731,946
Loss on remission of interest	861,650,555
Double principle interest	3,325,079,640
Receivable from RAKUB	1,564,990,206
Remission against 1st claim loan	50,684,233
Swaninver credits	5,246,766
Interest on loans <5,000 taka	647,298,437
Remissionable interest account	1,734,383,356
Waiver credits	79,241,162
Loan board credit	1,416,604
20% remission of classified >4 years	70,110,628
Fructional power pump loans	15,210,732
Legal expenses of written off loans	13,244,765
50% of loans <5,000 taka	7,999,943
Accrued interest receivable	1,380,255,074
Total	15,989,582,568

(3) Imbalance of 2 million taka between assets and liabilities and capital due to rounding

Table A4.2. BKB Recapitalization: Optimistic Scenario with 25 Percent of Standard Loans Carved Out

(based on 30 June 2005 balance sheet; millions of taka)

Item	Audited	Carve out bad assets	Adjusted	Recapitalize to 12% capital adequacy ratio	Recapitalized
Total liquid assets	6,802	0	6,802	0	6,802
Cash on hand	4,024		4,024		4,024
Deposits with other banks	2,778		2,778		2,778
Investments (1)	1,719	−1,716	3	38,988	38,991
Net loans and advance	65,673	−35,009	30,664	0	30,664
Standard	40,885	−10,221	30,664		30,664
Substandard	4,763	−4,763	0		0
Doubtful	4,738	−4,738	0		0
Loss	15,287	−15,287	0		0
Fixed assets	935		935		935
Other assets (2)	20,154	−15,990	4,164		4,164
Total assets (3)	**95,283**	**−52,715**	**42,568**	**38,988**	**81,557**
Total borrowings	34,243	−33,537	706	0	706
Borrowing from Bangladesh Bank	33,389	−33,389	0		0
Borrowing from government	148	−148	0		0
Borrowing from other banks	706		706		706
Deposits and bills payable	56,345		56,345		56,345
Other liabilities	20,216		20,216		20,216
Total liabilities	**110,804**	**−33,537**	**77,267**	**0**	**77,267**
Paid-up capital	2,400		2,400		2,400
Statutory reserves			0		0
Other reserves	1,305		1,305		1,305
Retained earnings	−19,224	−19,178	−38,402	38,988	587
Total capital	**−15,519**	**−19,178**	**−34,697**	**38,988**	**4,292**
Total liabilities and capital (3)	**95,285**	**−52,715**	**42,570**	**38,988**	**81,559**

Notes: See table A4.1. for notes.

Costs of Rehabilitating BKB

The cost to the government of rehabilitating BKB would have four components: the costs of repaying BKB's borrowing from Bangladesh Bank, of writing off BKB's borrowing from the government, of recapitalizing BKB, and of technical assistance to support the rehabilitation process ($5 million over three years) and new information technology systems ($15 million). If responsibility for collecting the loans carved out of BKB is transferred to a competent and appropriately motivated work-out company, there is some prospect of recovering amounts due from borrowers. In table A4.2 these are shown as reducing the net cost to the government of rehabilitating BKB, but it should be recognized that the costs of rehabilitation are certain and immediate, whereas the costs of recoveries are uncertain at best.

Costs of Recapitalizing RAKUB

Efforts to recapitalize RAKUB should aim to restore the bank to complete financial health. Tables A4.3 and A4.4 provide two scenarios for

Table A4.3. RAKUB Recapitalization: Realistic Scenario with 50 Percent of Standard Loans Carved Out

(based on 30 June 2005 balance sheet; millions of taka)

Item	Audited	Carve out bad assets	Adjusted	Recapitalize to 12% capital adequacy ratio	Recapitalized
Total liquid assets	2,891	0	2,891	0	2,891
Cash on hand	946		946		946
Deposits with other banks	1,945		1,945		1,945
Investments	3,450	−3,378	72	4,341	4,413
Net loans and advances	21,428	−13,918	7,510	0	7,510
Standard	15,020	−7,510	7,510		7,510
Substandard	869	−869	0		0
Doubtful	1,112	−1,112	0		0
Loss	4,427	−4,427	0		0
Fixed assets	65		65		65
Other assets (1)	2,552	−1,894	658		658
Total assets	**30,386**	**−19,190**	**11,196**	**4,341**	**15,537**
Total borrowings	15,949	−15,935	14	0	14
Borrowing from Bangladesh Bank	15,607	−15,607	0		0
Borrowing from BKB	328	−328	0		0
Borrowing from other banks	14		14		14
Deposits and bills payable	11,578		11,578		11,578

(continued)

Table A4.3. RAKUB Recapitalization: Realistic Scenario with 50 Percent of Standard Loans Carved Out *(continued)*

(based on 30 June 2005 balance sheet; millions of taka)

Item	Audited	Carve out bad assets	Adjusted	Recapitalize to 12% capital adequacy ratio	Recapitalized
Other liabilities	2,956		2,956		2,956
Total liabilities	**30,483**	**−15,935**	**14,548**	**0**	**14,548**
Paid-up capital	1,500		1,500		1,500
Statutory reserves	0		0		0
Other reserves	209		209		209
Retained earnings	−1,807	−3,255	−5,062	4,341	−721
Total capital	**−98**	**−3,255**	**−3,353**	**4,341**	**988**
Total liabilities and capital	**30,385**	**−19,190**	**11,195**	**4,341**	**15,536**

Notes:

(1) Other assets suspense adjustment for remission of interest

Crop loans	14,759
Loans <taka 5,000	469,846
Weavers credit	17,732,258
2% rebate	75,187
Pre-2004 agricultural loans	74,276,112
Double of principal interest	1,788,401,124
Weavers credit penalty interest	1,217,894
Swanirvar loans	1,801,872
Prakalpo loans	9,251,640
UNCDF loans	512,227
Obsolete notes	15,957
Total	1,893,768,876

Table A4.4. RAKUB Recapitalization: Optimistic Scenario with 25 Percent of Standard Loans Carved Out

(based on 30 June 2005 balance sheet; millions of taka)

Item	Audited	Carve out bad assets	Adjusted	Recapitalize to 12% capital adequacy ratio	Recapitalized
Total liquid assets	2,891	0	2,891	0	2,891
Cash on hand	946		946		946
Deposits with other banks	1,945		1,945		1,945
Investments	3,450	−3,378	72	1,036	1,108
Net loans and advances	21,428	−10,163	11,265	0	11,265
Standard	15,020	−3,755	11,265		11,265
Substandard	869	−869	0		0
Doubtful	1,112	−1,112	0		0
Loss	4,427	−4,427	0		0

Table A4.4. RAKUB Recapitalization: Optimistic Scenario with 25 Percent of Standard Loans Carved Out *(continued)*
(based on 30 June 2005 balance sheet; millions of taka)

Item	Audited	Carve out bad assets	Adjusted	Recapitalize to 12% capital adequacy ratio	Recapitalized
Fixed assets	65		65		65
Other assets (1)	2,552	−1,894	658		658
Total assets	**30,386**	**−15,435**	**14,951**	**1,036**	**15,988**
Total borrowings	15,949	−15,935	14	0	14
Borrowing from Bangladesh Bank	15,607	−15,607	0		0
Borrowing from BKB	328	−328	0		0
Borrowing from other banks	14		14		14
Deposits and bills payable	11,578		11,578		11,578
Other liabilities	2,956		2,956		2,956
Total liabilities	**30,483**	**−15,935**	**14,548**	**0**	**14,548**
Paid-up capital	1,500		1,500		1,500
Statutory reserves	0		0		0
Other reserves	209		209		209
Retained earnings	−1,807	500	−1,307	1,036	−270
Total capital	**−98**	**500**	**402**	**1,036**	**1,439**
Total liabilities and capital	**30,385**	**−15,435**	**14,950**	**1,036**	**15,987**

Notes: See table A4.1. for notes.

the recapitalization of RAKUB. The first is a realistic scenario where, based on a diagnostic audit, 50 percent of loans graded standard in June 2005 are found to be classifiable. The second is an optimistic scenario where only 25 percent of standard loans are found to be classifiable after a diagnostic audit. In both scenarios the entire portfolio of the bank's substandard or worse loans (after classification by a diagnostic audit) are carved out of the bank, leaving it with a fully performing (payments of principal and interest made on time) loan portfolio. Other items are also carved out:

- RAKUB's claims on the government that have not been met (3,378 million taka) are booked as investments.
- A wide variety of assets representing claims for remission of interest, principal waivers, capitalized losses, and miscellaneous items that appear to be of no value (1,894 million taka) are booked as other assets.

- RAKUB borrowing from Bangladesh Bank (15,607 million taka).
- RAKUB borrowing from BKB (323 million taka).[2]

The difference between the book value of the assets removed and the value of liabilities transferred results in a reduction of the bank's capital of 3,255 million taka in the realistic scenario and an increase (because more liabilities are carved out than assets) of 500 million taka in the optimistic scenario (with the difference between the two outcomes being caused by the reduced quantity of standard loans removed in the optimistic scenario).

After carving out bad assets and offsetting some of the cost to the bank of doing so by removing liabilities, RAKUB's capital is negative even in the optimistic scenario. To restore it to financial health, the bank would then be recapitalized to about a 12 percent capital adequacy ration with an injection of government bonds of 4,341 million taka in the realistic scenario and 1,036 million taka in the optimistic scenario. These calculations use a 12 percent capital adequacy ratio rather than the regulatory minimum of 9 percent to allow for the absorption of continued operating losses while RAKUB is restructured and to provide some scope for renewed lending, which would increase RAKUB's risk assets. The exact amount of capital needed would only be determined only after diagnostic work has been completed and a business plan prepared, but would not be less than the amounts shown in tables A4.3 and A4.4.

Costs of Rehabilitating RAKUB

The cost to the government of rehabilitating RAKUB would have four components: the costs of repaying RAKUB's borrowing from Bangladesh Bank, of repaying RAKUB's borrowing from BKB, of recapitalizing RAKUB, and of technical assistance to support the rehabilitation process ($5 million over three years) and new information technology systems ($10 million). If responsibility for collecting the loans carved out of RAKUB is transferred to a competent and appropriately motivated work-out company, there is some prospect of recovering amounts due from borrowers. In Table A4.4 these are shown reducing the net cost to the government of rehabilitating RAKUB, but it should be recognized that the costs of the rehabilitation process are certain and immediate, whereas the recoveries are uncertain at best.

Costs of Closing BKB and RAKUB

The consolidated costs of closing BKB and RAKUB are shown in table A4.5.

Table A4.5. BKB and RAKUB Consolidated Estimated Cost of Closure
(based on 30 June 2005 balance sheet; millions of taka)

Item	Audited	Estimated liquidation value of assets	
Total liquid assets	9,693	9,693	
Cash on hand	4,970	4,970	100%
Deposits with other banks	4,723	4,723	100%
Investments	5,169	5,169	100%
Net loans and advances	87,101	15,029	
Standard	55,905	13,976	25%
Substandard	5,632	563	10%
Doubtful	5,850	293	5%
Loss	19,714	197	1%
Fixed assets	1,000	1,000	100%
Other assets	22,706	20,435	90%
Total assets	**125,669**	**51,326**	
Claims on liquidation estate			
Borrowing from Bangladesh Bank	48,996		
Borrowing from government and BKB	476		
Borrowing from other banks	720		
Deposits and bills payable	67,923		
Other liabilities	23,172		
Total claims	**141,287**	100%	
Total government claims	117,067	83%	
Government and Bangladesh Bank claims	49,144		
Plus claim from repayment of deposits	67,923		
Liquidation value of assets	51,326		
Total government and Bangladesh Bank recovery	42,528		
Government cash costs			
Repayment of matured bonds	5,169		
Payment of waivers (other assets)	20,435		
Payment of deposits	67,923		
Loss to Bangladesh Bank	48,996		
Government loan to BKB	148		
Total cash loss	142,671		
Less: share of recovery	−42,528		
Net cost of liquidation to government and Bangladesh Bank	**100,143**		

Notes

1. A diagnostic audit involves an in-depth examination of the financial condition of a bank and assesses the quality of its systems, governance, management, and risk controls, among other things. The test applied by the diagnostic to loan classification is whether the borrower has the capacity and willingness to pay, so to be classified as standard a loan must be both current on payments of principal and interest as well as likely to remain so.

2. BKB does not record the same amount on its balance sheet, recording 1,565 million taka as receivable from RAKUB under other assets. This problem will have to be resolved during the diagnostic audit of the two banks.

Movable Collateral System

The use of movable collateral in Bangladesh is constrained by the following:

- The creation of security interests over movable assets is complex, lengthy, and relatively expensive.
- The priority of security interests over movable assets (that is, the public demonstration of the existence of such interests and the establishment of their priority) is unclear.
- The publicity of security interests over movable assets functions poorly.
- The enforcement of security interests for all assets is slow and expensive.

Creation of Security Interests

The creation of a security interest in a reformed system is quick and does not require excessive documentation. Reformed systems do not place restrictions on the type of property used in security agreement (such goods not yet created or intangible goods), nor are there restrictions on the agents who can enter into a security agreement (such as women, small businesses, or farmers). Reformed systems do not require assets to be specifically identified; rather, they allow for a general description of property (such as grain, petroleum, or cattle).[1] Security agreements can describe property in any way the borrower and secured lender agree.

The creation of security in Bangladesh is generally straightforward. There are no legal provisions governing the creation of security on movable property, since the creation of security interests in movable property is by contract, which is mainly governed by contract law.[2] Bangladeshi laws do not place limits on parties to a transaction or restrictions on the nature or type of property used in a security agreement, and they allow for a general description of properties.

A key constraint for the creation of a security interest lies in the long list of "security documents" required by creditors, without any apparent legal justification. There are six basic types of security documents that are commonly taken by banks and financial institutions in Bangladesh.[3] In addition, other documents are often required. There is no judicial precedent justifying any advantage to taking numerous documents. By contrast, with mortgage deeds a single short document suffices to create security, supplemented by statutory rights and obligations. A long list of documents invariably raises costs for drafting, preparing, reviewing, and custody, and lengthens the time it takes to create a security interest.

The creation of a security interest is a constraint to the extent that no uniform law covers all security devices, regardless of function. This severely restricts the ability of lenders to establish covenants based on the commercial interests of the creditor or the business, because some security interests are stronger than others.[4] Table A5.1 compares Bangladesh's system with reformed systems in terms of the creation of security interests.

Priority of Security Interests

A priority system is needed to distinguish rankings among those who might have a claim on property offered as collateral. Rules that establish priority among creditors also increase the likelihood that a secured lender will recover the value of collateral.[5] Clear rules for establishing priority among creditors permit lenders to assess a loan's potential risk and return based, among other things, on the value of collateral and the order of priority of other creditors. For example, an asset with a market value of 100,000 taka might provide sufficient collateral for a loan of 30,000 taka if there are no prior security interests, but not if there is a prior security interest of 90,000 taka.[6]

Table A5.1. Attributes of Creation in Secured Finance Systems in Bangladesh and Good Practice Environments

Feature	Good practices	Bangladesh practice	Examples of economic effects in Bangladesh
Coverage of goods and transactions	Allow security interest to be created by any lender and borrower in any present or futureproperty and in all transactions	Matches good practice	In general, goods that have economic importance and value may be used as collateral under the law
Rules on descriptions of collateral permit general (floating) descriptions, or there is no requirement to identify each good specifically	Allow the creditor and debtor to describe collateral any way they choose	Matches good practice	For most economic transactions, goods that could serve as collateral are difficult to identify specifically. Not necessary to track each specific item of collateral.
Description of collateral allows use of goods that may not currently exist	Permits all property, whether it exists or not, to serve as collateral for a loan	Does not explicitly prevent future property from serving as collateral. However, because of deficiencies in enforcement, in practice this becomes a very risky endeavor.	Increases the risk to lenders of securing goods that may not currently exist.

Source: Authors' analysis.

Bangladesh's laws for the priority system fall short in a number of areas. Each creditor has a preference to be the first in priority against others to rights to secured movable property.[7] But there are often competing creditors claiming rights to the movable property of a debtor,[8] and in such cases the laws do not offer clear guidance on priority. Moreover, there is no central and public point of reference to establish the priority of various creditors of a debtor.[9]

Firstly, there are no statutory rules of priority for charges filed with the Registrar of Joint Stock Companies and Firms and no case laws on priority of security interests on movable property or on the legal effect of security sharing agreements.[10] Thus priority among secured creditors is assessed on the rule of first in time (first party to file has priority), in a descending order of the time of creation of security interests. But even with the first in time rule, it is difficult to establish priority for a creditor—primarily because all searches of the registry are done manually, and with significant time lags. In fact, 21 days is permitted to file a charge document.[11]

Moreover, laws in Bangladesh are unclear about the superpriority of some creditors, such as the state, on tax liens allowing them priority over existing security interests that had been filed in the registry before they made their claims. Under such a system the law might grant secured creditors a ranking of priority based on the date they filed their security interest in the registry. But another law might give the state priority for taxes due regardless of when or even if the state filed a tax lien against the property serving as collateral. When the state's claim is not public, a potential lender cannot tell in advance whether property offered as collateral has tax claims against it. Because the lender's right against the collateral depends on a fact that is difficult for the lender to know—whether the borrower has any hidden tax liability—such systems undermine the purpose of collateral.[12]

In addition, in Bangladesh there are no clear priority rules for future advances or modifications to a charge filed with the Registrar of Joint Stock Companies and Firms. Such advances or modifications could include increasing the amount secured or adding new parties to the charge. In fact, many legal arguments in Bangladesh take the position that any modification to an existing charge puts it in a lower priority status relative to any charges filed after the original charge. This approach is perverse. In practice it means that in Bangladesh, if a creditor wanted to increase a credit line or a loan amount, and in doing so "modify" the original security agreement, the creditor would lose its original priority status. This structure makes it impossible for lenders to safely offer revolving credit lines secured by movable property to borrowers.[13]

Bangladesh's system often does not permit a security interest to continue in proceeds. For example, there is no legal provision (or clear case law) for security interests in movable property (raw materials) used in finished products. So, for example, if the security interest is an intermediary input, such as cotton, once the input is transformed into a garment, the security interest against the original cotton no longer applies. This poses a major risk to the lender. Once the chain of security interest is broken, the lender must negotiate a new security interest in the proceeds or products of the original collateral. If the borrower refuses to negotiate a new agreement, the lender must turn to the courts to collect.

In modern systems a security interest can continue in proceeds for an indefinite period or number of transactions, limited only by the ability to trace those proceeds. Lenders can be more confident of retaining their original priority. During the period of transformation the security interest would automatically attach to the cash received or to the finished product made from the secured input.

In companies' legislation there are no provisions on the priority of creditors in whose favor charges are registered with the Registrar of Joint Stock Companies and Firms in the distribution of payments in a company that is closing. Thus it is arguable that any payments made to a creditor at a time when a debtor is unable to pay its debts, as determined under the laws, may be the subject of actions by a receiver or liquidator to draw back such payments and have the same declared as fraudulent preferences.

The net outcome in the Bangladeshi system is that different security interest laws have different priority structures, creating confusion about the order of priority. When priority rules contradict one another, they compound the lenders' uncertainty and lower the value of the property as collateral. Table A5.2 compares Bangladesh's with reformed systems in terms of the assignment of priority.

Publicity of Security Interests

In any priority system there must be a place or means for making the security interest public. Otherwise the lender has no practical way of determining whether prior interests in property exist when advancing credit secured by that property.

Generally the two systems that are used are a registry system and a notice filing archive. The difference between them is that the registry system files actual copies of the security agreement or detailed abstracts of it, while the notice filing archives file only a notice of its existence.

Today's notice filing systems are usually Internet-based and allow potential lenders to quickly determine whether the property offered as collateral by a borrower has prior security interests or other encumbrances. The most modern systems provide Internet access to a database that anyone can search by any characteristic of lender, debtor, or collateral.[14]

In Bangladesh only charge documents of companies creating certain types of security interests are filed within 21 days of creation at the companies' registry, the office of the Registrar of Joint Stock Companies and Firms. The existing registry system raises substantial barriers to the publicity of security agreements.

Firstly, the system allows for the registry of security interests on movable property only for companies. In practice this means that most small businesses, which are sole proprietors, are effectively excluded from using their movable property to secure loans.

Second, there is no method of notification of security interests of all types, such as guarantees, hire purchases, conditional sales, or securitization,

Table A5.2. Attributes of Priority in Secured Finance Systems in Bangladesh and Good Practice Environments

Feature	Good practices	Bangladesh practice	Examples of economic effects in Bangladesh
Establishing priority	Allow a creditor or seller on credit to establish a ranking among those who might have a claim against property offered as collateral and make that ranking public. Use first-to-file basis to determine priority, and designate the place or means for making the security interest public.	Use first-to-file basis to determine priority but the archaic system of establishing priority in the registry (manual searches) makes it difficult to determine if there is a prior encumbrance.	Lenders cannot be sure of their priority until a manual search has occurred. Delays in this process make it risky and difficult for lenders, and considerably slow loan processing times for borrowers.
Rules for ranking superpriorities (such as tax claims and liens by the state)	Assign priority to tax claims, liens, and state debts based on the time of filing a notice in the public filing archive.	Does not set clear rules for ranking the priority of a security interest claim relative to a tax claim. May create conflict between secured claims of private creditors and priority given by law for state tax liens. Where state claims are not public, makes it impossible for potential lenders to tell in advance whether tax liens exist against collateral.	The state's ability to place its claims before those of private creditors, regardless of when or whether it filed the claims, dramatically undermines the secured lending system. Laws contradicting one another compound lenders' uncertainty and lower the value of property a collateral.
Priority rules for future advances	Set out priority rules for future advances For credit lines that are paid down and then drawn on again, extend the same priority to subsequent advances as was assigned to the initial advance.	Does not allow for any modifications to an existing charge without risking loss of priority to the lender.	Not possible for lenders to safely offer revolving credit lines to borrowers. Lending environment is less competitive since borrowers are essentially tied to one lender, because second or third lenders will be less secure about their priority status.

Continuation in proceeds of a security interest	Permit a security interest to continue indefinitely in proceeds (as when inventory is sold for cash or turned into a finished product)	There is no legal provision (or clear case law) for security interests in movable property (raw materials) used in finished products	Once a pledge asset is transformed (such as from fertilizer to grain or from grain to cash), the lender must go to court to get a new security interest in the transformed product
Limits for fixtures	Separate the framework for securing loans with movable property and fixtures from the framework for mortgaging the principal real estate	For movable property attached in some way to immovable property, there is only case law—that the intention of the landowner and occupier determines if the property remains the property of the occupier and does not form part of the occupier and so should be considered movable property. This issue affects temporary structures, machinery, and heavy equipment that are the subject of a charge granted by an occupier and installed on leased premises.	No lenders finance the purchase or sale on credit of fixtures without also having a first trust on real estate to which the fixtures are attached. No loans are likely for furnaces, generators, and the like.

Source: Authors' analysis.

or of interests that arise under legal provisions such as liens for government dues or sellers' unpaid dues, or for notices of actions of enforcement of security, or otherwise affecting the secured property.

Third, the transaction costs of accessing required documentation are quite high. In Bangladesh the registry tends to have long lines of people waiting to get a certificate attesting to the existence of security interests or other encumbrances. By statute the records at the Registrar of Joint Stock Companies and Firms are open for public inspection and copies of filings are available for a fee. But in practice access is only effective through facilitators—that is, people who regularly visit the registry and are acquainted with its officials.[15]

Fourth, the verification process is often lengthy. A comprehensive search of the records on a company at the Registrar of Joint Stock Companies and Firms is time consuming and cannot be done on a real-time basis. To start with, a period of 21 days is permitted for filing a charge document—substantially raising the risk for lenders who cannot be sure that other encumbrances on the security have not been placed, which would affect their expected priority status.

Fifth, the system is entirely paper-based, and requires a physical visit to the registry for filing or information retrieval.[16] In addition, the laws of evidence require corroboration of any documents that are not originals, with original signatures. This means that only "original" evidence is admissible—scanned copies hold no evidentiary weight or value. In practice this means that the transaction costs of filing are extremely high for borrowers. Not only must they provide original records to the filing office, but the state of the registry makes likely loss or damage to original documents.

Sixth, filing of security agreements can be costly. Currently, for charges filed with the Registrar of Joint Stock Companies and Firms, fees are levied relative to the value of the property secured.[17] This significantly increases costs where multiple charge documents are filed (such as separate letters of hypothecation for different types of property). Moreover, the registry accepts only cash payment of official fees.

Finally, filing security agreements takes a substantial amount of time. In contrast to the registry system in Bangladesh, modern systems are Internet-based. An entire filing system is served by one computer program on a Web-based server. Foreign and domestic lenders—anyone with Internet access—can search the filing system. Those with the right to file can write to the database by entering a password. Lenders can immediately check filings for correctness. Table A5.3 compares Bangladesh's system with reformed systems in terms of publicity.

Table A5.3. Attributes of Publicity in Secured Finance Systems in Bangladesh and Good Practice Environments

Feature	Good practices	Bangladesh practice	Examples of economic effects in Bangladesh
Cost, accessibility, and quality of the registry	Publicize security interest through a notice filing system that allows any potential lender to quickly determine whether collateral offered by a borrower has a prior security interest. Provide an Internet-based system for movable property collateral, allowing national and international access to notices of security interests. Maintain filing archives that are user friendly, low-cost, and quick (for example, the typical cost in North America is between $2.5–15.0 per registration). Require the filing of only minimal information about a security interest (name, description, date of filing). Permit but do not require the use of state and notary certifications.	Registry system is paper-based and relies on archaic methods of filing, retrieval, payment, and publicity. Time and cost associated with registry processes are unnecessarily long and deter potential borrowers and lenders. Excludes important classes of borrowers (sole proprietors) and important classes of security agreements.	When lenders do not have access to the registry system or cannot deal with long delays, they cannot verify their priority status. Filing becomes too costly relative to the value of loans, for both borrowers and creditors. Micro and small businesses are excluded from the registry, and so cannot exploit the benefits of a secured loan.
Advance filing and blocking	Permit advance filings and reservation of a ranking of priority ("blocking")	Has no system for advance filings or for reservation of a ranking or priority. Allows lender 21 days to file a charge, which becomes effective from the time of the delivery with the intention to create a charge on a property.	Between the time a lender checks for prior encumbrances against a potential borrower's collateral and the time it grants the loan, another party could file a more senior security interest against the same collateral.
Unified or multiple systems of establishing priority	Apply one system of priorities to all security interests and to all other transaction undertaken for security, including leases and conditional sales.	Does not have a comprehensive priority system for all secured transactions.	Potential lenders that wish to take property as collateral need to check more than one system to learn of other encumbrances against the collateral.

Source: Authors' analysis.

Enforcement of Security Interests

The faster and more cheaply that property can be seized and sold, the more value it has as collateral. Unreformed systems present many barriers to rapid seizure and sale of collateral after a borrower defaults on a secured loan. This poses particular problems for movable property that depreciates rapidly (such as storable agricultural commodities).

Modern systems permit private repossession of collateral as long as it does not breach the peace. Generally this means that creditors cannot use force against debtors or break into private property. That usually allows a creditor's agents to take motor vehicles from public parking areas or haul away equipment from farms or open construction sites.

Under modern systems, if the creditor alleges that payment has not been made and shows proof of its security interest, a judge must issue an order to repossess. The debtor need not be present. Modern systems usually give the creditor far more rights than do unreformed systems, though they also levy very large penalties against creditors who abuse this process. Private repossession allows the debtor and the creditor to agree on alternative collection measures if the debtor should default.[18]

After seizure, modern systems also permit the creditor to sell the collateral as long as it conducts the sale in a commercially reasonable manner—and provide severe penalties for breaching this obligation. These systems place the responsibility for sale in the hands of those with the greatest incentive to maximize the value of the collateral and not divert proceeds to other uses. They give detailed instructions on how the creditor should return to the debtor any balance remaining after the collateral is sold and the loan is paid.

In Bangladesh, where enforcement is carried out by the courts and executed by the police, the process is estimated to take between one and three years—by which time most movable property will have lost all or most of its value. Lenders report problems at all stages of the process. This is true both for institutions that can avail themselves of the enforcement process through money loan courts and for those that have to use mainstream enforcement procedures.

Financial institutions that are not regulated by Bangladesh Bank follow the general method of enforcement of contracts for security interests. This means that the debtor would be filing before a subordinate court a lawsuit for the debt secured (a "money suit"), and if judgment is awarded in favor of the creditor and the debtor fails to pay, another lawsuit

Table A5.4. Attributes of Enforcement in Secured Finance Systems in Bangladesh and Good Practice Environments

Feature	Good practices	Bangladesh practice	Examples of economic effects in Bangladesh
Time frame for enforcing procedures	Allow harmless repossession and creditor-administered sale of collateral. Through civil procedure law, provide for ex parte court orders (can be issued even if debtor is not present)	Relies on complex, court-administered systems of appraisal and auction of collateral. May forbid sale of collateral for less than amount of loan.	Because enforcement (seizure and sale) takes one to three years, it makes most classes of movable property (accounts receivable, perishable goods) useless as collateral because they do not maintain their economic value. With costly court-administered sales, lenders do not get paid and nothing is left over for debtors.
Seizure of collateral	Allow only proof that debt payment has been made as defense against seizure. Have some homestead or exempt property provisions.	Requires that secured party have a court order for seizure. Permits many challenges to the legal process, each of which can delay the order for seizure. With a court order for seizure, requires that court police seize property—but there is a low priority for rapid execution. Documents must be filed in multiple courts when property is geographically dispersed.	Costs and delays associated with seizure of property drastically reduce the value of property once it has been seized. Makes it less likely for a lender to rely on seizure as a final recourse, and so less likely to accept movable property as collateral.
Sale of collateral	Give parties freedom to agree on terms of sale for collateral. Require creditors to notify debtors and junior secured creditors before sale of collateral. Allow creditors to retain collateral in complete satisfaction of secured debt; does not place restrictions on amount for which collateral can be sold (strict foreclosure).	Relies on complex, court-administered systems of appraisal and auction of collateral.	Because enforcement (seizure and sale) takes one to three years, it makes most classes of movable property (accounts receivable, perishable goods) useless as collateral because they do not maintain their economic value.

Source: Authors' analysis.

(an "execution case") is filed for the sale of secured property. Execution cases are filed in courts with geographic jurisdiction where the property is located. Where movable property is situated in various locations, this requirement can result in the filing of such cases in several courts. Court fees are payable at rates based on the amounts or value of the property claimed—making enforcement against multiple or highly valued properties prohibitively expensive.

Moreover, court processes have uncertain outcomes because judges' interpretation of the laws can differ substantially.[19] To alleviate delays in the system, a special law was enacted in 2003 under which special courts (money loan courts) operate to hear lawsuits for debt recovery by institutions regulated by Bangladesh Bank.

Any judgment of such a court is still enforced by filing an execution case. But where a hypothecation of movable property is taken with a power of attorney to sell the property, the creditor is to sell the hypothecated property, set off the sale proceeds against the outstanding debt, and then initiate legal proceedings for recovery of the remaining debt. This process is designed to greatly expedite enforcement against outstanding debts since courts are required to issue judgments within three months of filing.

But in practice the ability of financial institutions to proceed to sell is usually obstructed by the absence of the property or because such actions are suspended (stayed) by judicial order because of a challenge from the debtor. In fact, any allegation of unlawful action by a court can be challenged by filing petitions for judicial review by the Supreme Court of Bangladesh, and hearings of the debt recovery case are stayed until such hearings and any appeals filed are settled.[20]

Finally, another source of delay is the reliance on police—court police or ordinary public police—to enforce orders for repossession. These police forces are understaffed and undermotivated.

In the end, unreformed laws provide for complex and multitiered systems for appraisal and auction of collateral administered by courts. The procedures are long and slow, and often other laws and regulations impose other impediments—such as forbidding the sale of collateral for less than the amount of a loan. Designed to protect debtors, the laws fail: court fees, attorneys, and auctioneers absorb most of the value, and lenders do not get fully paid. In the end, nothing is left over for debtors regardless. And creditors assign very little real value to movable property as collateral, given that it may be impossible to enforce a debt against it in the long term. Table A5.4 compares Bangladesh's system with reformed systems in terms of enforcement.

Notes

1. Limiting the enforceability of security interests to collateral that has been specifically identified means that a security interest in general inventories, such as wheat or appliances, cannot "float" to new inventories once the original goods have been sold (Fleisig, Safavian, and de la Pena 2006).

2. Pledges (delivery of possession but no transfer of title to movable property) are the exception—they are the only security agreement governed by statute. But pledges cannot be registered in the Registrar of Joint Stock Companies and Firms.

3. These documents include demand promissory notes (together with letters of continuation), letters or deeds of hypothecation (together with power of attorney to sell the property), letters or deeds of pledge, letters of lien and setoff (relating to bank accounts), and guarantees.

4. For example, a pledge has priority over other nonpossessory security interests because of possession by the creditor.

5. This is in contrast to an unsecured creditor, who must go to court to enforce an unsecured loan and get a judgment lien that calls for seizing the property of the debtor and selling it to satisfy debt.

6. This section draws heavily on Fleisig, Safavian, and de la Pena (2006).

7. Although bankruptcy legislation uses the term secured creditor, there is no definition of the term.

8. Their priority to claim and enforce their rights may arise by contract, by operation of law, or from specific statutory provisions.

9. Examples of competing creditors are tax authorities for alleged arrears of taxes, lenders for debts due, suppliers of unpaid-for goods to the debtor, receivers in bankruptcy, and judgment creditors to enforce court decrees awarded in their favor.

10. This refers to a situation when there are several secured creditors with bilateral or multilateral charges of a debtor, who all seek first priority. In such a situation an intercreditor agreement (conventionally called a "security sharing agreement") is entered into among creditors whereby they agree that the charges rank on an equal basis, the proceeds of enforcement are to be shared in proportion, and each creditor's secured amount bears to the aggregate outstandings of all the creditors. Although security sharing agreements are common practice, their validity has yes to be tested in Bangladesh.

11. Although such filings take effect from the date of such documents.

12. Similar problems arise from giving superpriority to debts to the state, including loan payments due state banks. Superpriority allows the state to execute judgment liens against the debtors' property ahead of the security interests of private creditors, even when those state liens were filed later than the security interests or not filed at all.

13. Correctly applied, the unreformed law would permit a borrower to pay off a credit line that had first priority, take out a new loan secured with the same collateral, and then draw again on the second credit line. This transaction, a future advance against the credit line, would place the first lender in second position even though that lender had filed first. Lenders, understanding this, rarely offer secured loans as lines of credit.

14. Modern systems do not file the entire agreement or even a substantial extract. Instead they file only minimal information about the security interest—a notice of its existence that typically includes only the names and addresses of the parties, a description of the collateral, and the date and time of filing. Filing less information eases concerns about allowing greater public access to the filing system, lowers filing costs, and simplifies the registration system. Of course, this abbreviated information may not tell a potential lender enough to decide whether to accept a potential borrower's property as collateral. But the filing system gives the lender the information needed to inquire privately about additional details in loan contracts. If potential borrowers refuse to supply that information, lenders are free to refuse their loan application (Fleisig, Safavian, and de la Pena 2006).

15. Further, contrary to statutory provisions and judicial decisions, the registry often declines to provide copies of filings without its review of other filings and documents. But if the registry finds filings satisfactory, after such "acceptance" certified copies of filings are available at ad hoc fees.

16. Even with an upcoming computerization project supported by the South Asia Enterprise Development Facility, the computer systems will be desktop- or network-based. Such systems require a great deal of maintenance and training of operators and are unsuitable for use by the general public.

17. Government fees for registration of a charge with the registry are 600 taka for the first 10 million taka secured by the charge (amount secured as stated in the charge instrument, not the value of the underlying asset) and 410 taka for each 10 million taka secured thereafter.

18. In keeping with the voluntary nature of such agreements, the law should specifically forbid creditors from using the assistance of any government official without a court order.

19. There is no special legislation or procedure for access to, seizure, and sale of secured movable property, except for pledges.

20. Yet despite all such factors, proceedings at money loan courts are still swifter than those at ordinary civil courts where creditors in Bangladesh (other than banks and financial institutions) are to have recourse. Money loan courts are only available to regulated formal financial intermediaries.

Case Studies of Six Microfinance Institutions

To understand what is holding back the scaling up of microfinance lending to MSMEs and MSMFs, six case studies were conducted of microfinance institutions lending to the sector. The case studies focused on the strengths and weaknesses of the institutions' innovative products, the efficiency and profitability achieved in delivering them, and the scope for and challenges faced by other microfinance institutions in replicating their experience.

Methodology

The field work for this research was conducted between May and July 2006, and each of the six cases involved a review of various program and financial documents; interviews with loan officers, branch managers, senior managers, and other staff; interviews with clients of the institutions; and observations of field operations.

Selection of Institutions

The microfinance institutions were selected based on three criteria:

- Innovativeness of products in terms of client groups, loan terms and conditions, and/or delivery mechanisms.

- Size of program—that is, products with significant outreach in terms of members and portfolio size were selected, while tiny pilot projects were not considered even if they were innovative.
- Potential for replication of the product based on current size, expansion plans of provider(s), and number of microfinance institutions offering the same or similar services.

The Six Selected Institutions

The six selected MFIs—three for agricultural finance and three for microenterprise finance—were:

- Samaj O Jathi Gathan (SOJAG), which is innovative in terms of target group and loan portfolio, terms, conditions, and delivery. It offers cash loans to MSMFs for crop production (mainly rice) in two seasons a year. It disburses loans in a single installment at the beginning of the planting season and recovers them in one installment after the harvest. SOJAG also organizes farmers into groups that meet once a month to deposit their small savings and share agricultural information.
- The Center for Action Research–Barind (CARB),[1] which is innovative in terms of target group and loan portfolio, terms, conditions, and delivery. It offers in-kind loans to marginal and small male farmers through a network of agricultural input sellers during the two production seasons each year. The center organizes farmers into groups based on the locations of deep tube wells used for irrigation. But unlike regular microcredit programs, no group meetings are held.
- Bangladesh Extension Education Services (BEES), which has extended its group-based credit methodology to provide financial services to small and marginal farmers, mainly women. BEES loans are used for poultry, livestock, fisheries, crops, horticulture, and related trades. More than 30 microfinance institutions that receive financing from PKSF follow this approach, and BEES is representative of the sector.
- The Progoti (formerly Micro Enterprise Lending and Assistance) program of BRAC (one of the three largest microfinance institutions in Bangladesh), which offers loans to individual microentrepreneurs who are mostly nonpoor and are not former microcredit borrowers. BRAC created this loan product and takes land as collateral against loans.
- The Small Business Loan (SBL) and Small Entrepreneurs Loan (SEL) programs offered by ASA (another of the three largest microfinance institutions in Bangladesh). SBL products are offered to shop owners

using a group lending methodology, while SEL products are offered to manufacturing enterprises using individual lending. Most borrowers under both programs are new clients and not former borrowers from ASA's regular microcredit program.

- The Sustainable Refinancing for Enterprises and Technological Improvement (SREESTI) program of PMUK (Padakhep Manobik Unnayan Kendra, which means Padakhep Center for Human Development), which—along with more than 100 PKSF partner microfinance institutions—finances graduates of regular microcredit program who need larger loans and are willing to continue the group-based system. PMUK mostly finances female entrepreneurs who have been participants in its microcredit program for several years.

Lending by the Six Institutions

The selected microfinance institutions are roughly representative of total microfinance lending to MSMEs and MSMFs (table A6.1). Details on the products they offer to MSMFs are provided in table A6.2, while products for MSMEs are shown in table A6.3.

Financial Performance of the Six Institutions

None of the six microfinance institutions had management information systems that allowed them to calculate product profitability. So, this section analyzes the institutions' overall profitability.

The three MFIs engaged in lending to MSMFs are financially sustainable, as their financial self-sufficiency values were greater than 100 percent in 2006 and they reported positive (though low) returns on assets (table A6.4). Their loan portfolios are also in good condition, as measured by high loan recovery rates. The obvious weakness revealed in these performance data is the comparatively small number of active borrowers and outstanding loans per loan officer. This could be due to a slow buildup in the agricultural portfolio after hiring loan officers to market loans, the seasonal nature of agricultural lending, or lending technologies and management systems that are not conducive to high levels of staff efficiency. All three of these institutions offer some nonfinancial services to their borrowers, which may also absorb some of the time that loan officers could otherwise devote to managing more borrowers and larger portfolios. Efficiency and profitability need to be improved over time in these institutions; fortunately, trends have been positive in recent years.

Table A6.1. Activities of the Six Selected Microfinance Institutions

Institution	Outreach	Number of MSME and MSMF borrowers	Lending approach for MSMEs and MSMFs	Services offered	Estimated number of microfinance institutions in the same category	Constraints faced by microfinance in institutions this category
SOJAG	Small, less than 20,000 clients	4,300	Group loans for men	Mainly financial services, with limited extension services	47, with total potential of around 200	Little experience in lending to men. Reluctance to make bullet payment loans. Consider crop loans to be high risk. May offer only seasonal loans for cattle fattening. Cap on borrowers' landholding limits growth in loan size. Limited staff skills.
CARB	Small, 20,000 borrowers	20,000	Individual, in-kind loans for men	Loans, with limited extension services	Unique	Additional transaction costs for making in-kind loans. Other constraints similar to previous category.

BEES	Small to medium-size, about 100,000 clients	12,000 in two projects	Group loans, mostly for women	Primarily financial services, with some nonfinancial services (such as training on crop, feed, poultry, and livestock production; distribution of vegetable seeds twice a year; monthly medical checkups).	25, with total potential of around 250	Limited capital for growth. Offer no nonfinancial services. Early stage of development induces cautious approach to expansion.
BRAC	Very large, millions of clients	225,000 cumulative borrowers; 92,000 outstanding borrowers	Individual	Financial only	Unique	Require collateral for loans. Perception of limited supply of good clients.
ASA	Very large, millions of clients	Almost 200,000 for two products	Individual and group	Financial only	Unique	Early stage of development induces cautious approach to expansion. Limited number of production-oriented enterprises available as potential clients.

(continued)

Table A6.1. Activities of the Six Selected Microfinance Institutions (continued)

Institution	Outreach	Number of MSME and MSMF borrowers	Lending approach for MSMEs and MSMFs	Services offered	Estimated number of microfinance institutions in the same category	Constraints faced by microfinance institutions in this category
PMUK	Small to medium-size, more than 100,000 clients	5,200 members; 4,500 borrowers	Group	Primarily financial, with limited nonfinancial services.	100, with total potential of around 200 in two or three years	Limited staff skills. Limited capital for growth. Early stage of development induces cautious approach to expansion. Loans limited to graduates. More robust lending methodology required before major expansion.

Source: Authors' analysis.

Table A6.2. Loan Products for MSMFs

Institution	Target clients	Loan amounts	Interest rate (flat rate)[a]	Type of loan management	Collateral requirement	Guarantor required?	Group meetings	Duration of loan; type of payments
SOJAG	Farmers cultivating 0.5–2.5 acres, especially rice, in Dhamrai subdistrict, north of Dhaka	Linked to amount of land cultivated; maximum of 9,000 taka	Annual effective rate of 15% paid in one installment	Group-based; loans made to individuals	None	Yes	Monthly meetings; priority for attending at beginning of the crop season and at harvest	Production season of five or six months; paid in one installment after harvest
CARB	Poor farmers using deep tube wells in the Barind Tract, in northwestern Bangladesh. Loans are largely for rice production	In-kind loans covering production inputs; averaged 4,410 taka in 2006	Interest charged on each purchase order until repayment at 0.80 taka per 1,000 taka, for an annual effective rate of 29.2%	Groups formed by farmers using the same well; loans made to individuals	None	No	None	Production season of five to eight months; paid in one or two installments after harvest

(continued)

Table A6.2. Loan Products for MSMFs (continued)

Institution	Target clients	Loan amounts	Interest rate (flat rate)[a]	Type of loan management	Collateral requirement	Guarantor required?	Group meetings	Duration of loan; type of payments
BEES	Poor women from households farming 0.5–2.5 acres engaged in crop, livestock, and poultry activities in northwestern Bangladesh	12,000–25,000 taka	12.5% with weekly payments, for an annual effective rate of 25%	Group-based; loans made to individuals	None	No	Weekly meetings for financial transactions and to deliver other services	One year; 45 weekly installments

Source: Authors' analysis.

a. Several microfinance institutions express their interest rates as flat rates—that is, computing interest on the original face amount of the loan, rather than on the declining balances that actually remain in the borrower's hands as successive installments of principal are repaid. The total principal and interest is then amortized over several weeks or months. The annual effective rate becomes roughly twice the quoted rate.

Table A6.3. Loan Products for MSMEs

Institution	Target clients	Loan amounts	Interest rate (flat rate)[a]	Type of loan management	Collateral requirement	Guarantor required?	Group meeting	Duration of loan; type of payments
ASA (SBL and SEL)	Small businesses (shops/trading) for SBL; production-type enterprises for SEL	SBL: first loan cycle is 15,000–50,000 taka; successive loans increase by 5,000 taka. SEL: 30,000–300,000 taka	SBL: 15% SEL: 12.5%	Group-based for SBL (10–15 people per group); individual lending for SEL	None	For SEL, third party guarantee required	Loan collection meeting for SBL; no meetings for SEL. SEL clients repay individually at branch offices or loan officers collects payments at clients' premises	One year; monthly installments
BRAC (Progoti)	All types of microenterprises; mostly shop owners and traders	50,000–300,000 taka	15%	Loans made to individuals	Land as collateral (except for female entrepreneurs which borrow 50,000 taka). Equitable mortgage deed is signed.	Yes	None. Clients repay individually at branch offices	One year; monthly installments

(continued)

Table A6.3. Loan Products for MSMEs *(continued)*

Institution	Target clients	Loan amounts	Interest rate (flat rate)[a]	Type of loan management	Collateral requirement	Guarantor required?	Group meeting	Duration of loan; type of payments
PMUK (SREESTI)	Graduates of microcredit programs	20,000– 300,000 taka	12.5%	Group-based, loans made to individuals	None	Yes	Weekly meetings as a part of regular microcredit group	One year; weekly installments

Source: Authors' analysis.

a. ASA, BRAC, and PKSF partner organizations express their interest rates as flat rates—that is, computing interest on the original face amount of the loan, rather than on the declining balances that actually remain in the borrower's hands as successive installments of principal are repaid. The total principal and interest is then amortized over several weeks or months. The annual effective rate becomes roughly twice the quoted rate.

Table A6.4. Financial Viability Indicators for SOJAG, CARB, and BEES, 2005–06

Indicator	SOJAG		CARB		BEES	
	2005	2006	2005	2006	2005	2006
Profitability						
Operational self-sufficiency (percent)	151.1	175.4	85.4	132.6	121.9	124.5
Financial self-sufficiency (percent)	99.4	120.8	74.9	106.8	100.4	101.3
Return on assets (percent)	−0.19	0.25	−3.23	0.70	0.01	0.06
Other indicators						
Number of clients per loan officer	269	382	205	185	177	266
Number of borrowers per loan officer	134	227	205	185	142	220
Average loan size (taka)	7,527	7,111	3,965	4,410	6,666	6,149
Portfolio per loan officer (millions of taka)	0.73	1.36	0.22	0.34	0.56	0.94
Loan recovery rate (percent)	99.9	99.8	100	100	99.0	99.0

Source: Authors' analysis based on data provided by SOJAG, CARB, and BEES.
Note: Data are as of June for each year. These indicators are for the institutions' entire portfolios, not just their special agricultural loans. When investment income is excluded, the institutions may not be able to cover costs.

Among the microfinance institutions engaged in lending to MSMEs, ASA is the most profitable not only in this group but also in the industry—as indicated by 2005 profitability indicators of operational self-sufficiency (275 percent), financial self-sufficiency (170 percent), and return on assets (10.7 percent; table A6.5). These levels reflect efficiency gains achieved over the years and are reflected in ASA's number of borrowers per loan officer (441), portfolio per loan officer (1.78 million taka) and interest rate. ASA is followed by BRAC in terms of profitability. PMUK is less profitable than the two other, much larger organizations; its financial performance has suffered due to low efficiency factors and a lower interest rate.

Growth Prospects of the Six Institutions

All six of the microfinance institutions studied face constraints in expanding into their market segments, and the smaller ones are especially constrained by limited human and financial resources. Because farm sizes are largely fixed, there is limited scope for expanding lending to marginal, small, and medium-size farmers by increasing the average size of crop

Table A6.5. Financial Viability Indicators for ASA, BRAC, and PMUK, Various Years

Indicator	ASA		BRAC		PMUK	
	2004	2005	2004	2005	2005	2006
Profitability						
Operational self-sufficiency (percent)	244.6	275.2	207.10	196.13	142.24	127.72
Financial self-sufficiency (percent)	158.5	169.7	116.75	130.65	109.12	101.39
Return on assets (percent)	90.57	10.71	3.39	5.80	6.43	4.10
Other indicators						
Number of clients per loan officer	430	631	353	394	126	170
Number of borrowers per loan officer	397	441	281	341	117	150
Average loan size (taka)	7517	7129	7,326	8,350	8,959	10,273
Portfolio per loan officer (millions of taka)	1.72	1.78	1.06	1.42	0.595	0.872
Loan recovery rate (percent)	99.2	99.19	99.32	99.49	99.90	99.61

Source: Authors' analysis based on data provided by SOJAG, CARB, and BEES.
Note: Data are as of December for ASA and BRAC and as of June for PMUK. These indicators are for the institutions' entire portfolios, not just their special loans to micro, small, and medium-size enterprises.

loans. This is a major constraint on the profitability of the agricultural lenders. To minimize this problem, these microfinance institutions need to develop the capacity to make a wider range of agricultural loans (such as for equipment) and not limit their lending to seasonal loans for rice. But this change requires that they improve loan officer knowledge about a broader range of enterprises and upgrade their credit appraisal capacity.

The institutions lending to MSMEs also face constraints on expanding lending. Outside bazaars, a limited number of enterprises in any geographic area fit their lending criteria. Moreover, the smaller institutions have limited their lending to successful graduates of their traditional microfinance programs, which limits their potential pool of borrowers.

Note

1. The Barind Tract is a semi-arid dry area comprising several northwestern districts of Bangladesh.

Bibliography

Ananth, Bindu, Bastavee Barooah, Rupalee Ruchismita, and Aparna Bhatnagar. 2004. "A Blueprint for the Delivery of Comprehensive Financial Services to the Poor in India." Working paper. Center for Microfinance. Chennai, India. [http://ifmr.ac.in/pdf/ workingpapers/9/blueprint.pdf].

AXCO. 2006. "Insurance Market Report: Bangladesh (Property and Casualty)." AXCO Insurance Services Ltd, London.

Bangladesh Bank. 2004. "Prudential Regulation for Small Enterprise Financing [as amended by subsequent circulars]." Dhaka, Bangladesh.

————. 2006a. *Annual Report, 2005–06.* Dhaka, Bangladesh.

————. 2006b. "Banking Regulation and Policy Department Circular 5." Dhaka, Bangladesh.

————. 2006c. "Financial Sector Review." Dhaka, Bangladesh.

————. Various years. "Scheduled Banks Statistics, April-June." Dhaka, Bangladesh.

Bangladesh Bureau of Statistics 1999. "Census of Agriculture 1996: National Series, Volume 1." Dhaka, Bangladesh.

————. 2000a. "Household and Income Expenditure Survey." Dhaka, Bangladesh.

————. 2000b. *Yearbook of Agricultural Statistics of Bangladesh.* Dhaka, Bangladesh.

————. 2004. "Labour Force Survey: 2002–2003." Dhaka, Bangladesh.

Basu, Priya. 2006. "Improving Access to Finance for India's Rural Poor." World Bank, Washington, D.C.

Beck, T., and R. Levine. 2004. "Stock Markets, Banks and Growth: Panel Evidence." *Journal of Banking and Finance* 28 (3): 423–42.

Beck, T., A. Demirguc-Kunt, and S. Martinez Peria. 2004. "Finance, Inequality and Poverty: Cross-country Evidence." Policy Research Working Paper 3338. World Bank, Washington, D.C.

———. 2005. "Reaching Out: Access to and Use of Banking Services across Countries." Policy Research Working Paper 3754. World Bank, Washington, D.C.

———. 2006. "Banking Services for Everyone? Barriers to Bank Access around the World." Policy Research Working Paper 4079. World Bank, Washington, D.C.

BKB (Bangladesh Krishi Bank). 2005. *Annual Report*. Dhaka, Bangladesh.

Buchenau, Juan. 1997. "Financing Small Farmers in Latin America." Paper presented at the First Annual Seminar on New Development Finance, Frankfurt University, Germany.

Buchenau, Juan, and Richard L. Meyer. 2007. "Introducing Rural Finance into an Urban Microfinance Institution: The Example of Banco ProCredit El Salvador." Paper presented at the International Conference on Rural Finance Research: Moving Results into Policies and Practice, Food and Agriculture Organization, 19–21 March, Rome.

Christen, Robert Peck. 2000. "Commercialization and Mission Drift: The Transformation of Microfinance in Latin America." CGAP Occasional Paper 5. Consultative Group to Assist the Poor, Washington, D.C.

Churchill, Craig F. 1999. *Client-Focused Lending: The Art of Individual Lending*. Toronto: Calmeadow.

Daniels, Lisa. 2003. "National Private Sector Study of Enterprises in Bangladesh." Prepared for U.K. Department of International Development, U.S. Agency for International Development, Swiss Agency for Development and Cooperation, and Swedish International Development Cooperation Agency. Dhaka, Bangladesh.

Dellien, Hans, and Olivia Leland. 2006. "Introducing Individual Lending." Women's World Banking, New York.

Dellien, Hans, Jill Burnett, Anna Ginchermann, and Elizabeth Lynch. 2005. "Product Diversification in Microfinance: Introducing Individual Lending." Women's World Banking, New York.

Dyer, Jay, J. Peter Morrow, and Robin Young. 2004. "Case Study: The Agricultural Bank of Mongolia." Presented at the Scaling Up Poverty Reduction Conference, March, Shanghai.

Finmark Trust. 2003. "Access to Financial Services in Lesotho." Finmark Trust Research Paper 2. Johannesburg, South Africa.

Firpo, Janine. 2005. "HP's Remote Transaction System: A Technology Solution to Scale Microfinance." United Nations Capital Development Fund, New York. [http://www.uncdf.org/english/microfinance/pubs/newsletter/pages/2005_05/news_hp.php].

Fleisig, Heywood, Mehnaz Safavian, and Nuria de la Pena. 2006. "Reforming Collateral Laws to Increase Access to Finance." World Bank, Washington, D.C.

Gine, Xavier, Robert Townsend, and James Vickery. 2007. "Patterns of Rainfall Insurance Participation in Rural India." Presented at the Conference on Access to Finance, March, Washington, D.C.

Gonzalez-Vega, Claudio, Jorge Rodriguez-Meza, and Rafael Pleitez-Chaves. 2002. "Characteristicas de los clientes rurales de la Financiera Calpia: breve analysis." [http://aede.ag.ohio-state.edu/programs/RuralFinance/pdf/BASISfinal.pdf].

Hewlett-Packard. 2005. "Remote Transaction System." Solution Brief. Palo Alto, Calif. [http://www.hp.com/e-inclusion/en/project/microfin_brief.pdf].

Holden, Paul, and Prokopenko Vassili. 2001. "Financial Development and Poverty Alleviation: Issues and Policy Implications for Developing Countries." IMF Working Paper 01/160. International Monetary Fund, Washington, D.C.

Honohan, P. 2005. "Measuring Microfinance Access: Building on Existing Cross-country Data." Policy Research Working Paper 3606. World Bank, Washington, D.C.

Hossain, Mahabub, Manik Bose, Alamgir Chowdhury, and Ruth Meinzen-Dick. 2002. "Changes in Agrarian Relations and Livelihoods in Rural Bangladesh: Insights from Repeat Village Studies." In V. K.Ramachandran and M. Swaminathan, eds., Agrarian Studies: Essays on Agrarian Relations in Less-Developed Countries. New Delhi, India: Tulika Books.

Ibarra, H., and O. Mahul. 2004. "Self-Insurance Funds as Agriculture Insurance Providers: The Case of Fondos in Mexico." World Bank, Washington, D.C.

INAFI (International Network of Alternative Financial Institutions). 2007. "Reducing Vulnerability of the Poor through Social Security Products: A Market Survey on Microinsurance in Bangladesh." Research paper. Dhaka, Bangladesh.

IPC (Internationale Projekt Consult). 2006. "Building Up Capacities for Successful Lending to Micro, Small and Medium-sized Businesses." Presented at the Up-scaling SME Lending: New Tools seminar, organized by Small Industries Development Bank of India (SIDBI), September, New Delhi, India.

Ivatury, Gautam. 2006. "Using Technology to Build Inclusive Financial Systems." CGAP Focus Note 32. Consultative Group to Assist the Poor, Washington, D.C.

Khalily, M. A. Baqui, M. A. Taslim, Mahamood Osman Iman, and Salahuddin Ahmed Khan. 2002. "Impact of Formal Credit on Agricultural Production in Bangladesh." University of Dhaka, Bureau of Business Research, Dhaka, Bangladesh.

King, R. G., and R. Levine. 1993. "Finance and Growth: Schumpeter Might Be Right." *Quarterly Journal of Economics* 108 (3): 717–38.

Levine, R., N. Loayza, and T. Beck. 2000. "Financial Intermediation and Growth: Causality and Causes." *Journal of Monetary Economics* 46 (1): 31–77.

Lyman, Timothy, Gautam Ivatury, and Stefan Staschen. 2006. "Use of Agents in Bankless Banking for the Poor: Rewards, Risks and Regulation." CGAP Focus Note 38. Consultative Group to Assist the Poor, Washington, D.C.

Manuamorn, Ornsaran Pomme. 2005. "Scaling Up Micro-Insurance: The Case of Weather Insurance for Smallholders in India." World Bank, Commodity Risk Management Group, Washington, D.C.

Navajas, Sergio, and Claudio Gonzalez-Vega. 2003. "Financiera Calpia in El Salvador: Innovative Approaches to Rural Lending." In Mark D. Wenner, Javier Alvarado, and Francisco Galarza, eds., *Promising Practices in Rural Finance: Experiences from Latin America and the Caribbean*. Washington, D.C.: Inter-American Development Bank. [http://aede.ag.ohio-state.edu/programs/RuralFinance/pdf/eso2571.pdf].

RAKUB (Rajshahi Krishi Unnayan Bank). 2005. *Annual Report*. Rajshahi, Bangladesh.

Sa-Dhan. 2006. "Slide by Slide: A Slice of Microfinance Sector in India 2006." India. [http://www.sa-dhan.net/ResMaterials/SidebySideASliceof MicrofinanceOperationsinIndia2006.pdf].

Safavian, Mehnaz, Heywoood Fleisig, and Jevgenijs Steinbuks. 2006. "Unlocking Dead Capital: How Reforming Collateral Laws Improves Access to Finance." Viewpoint 307. World Bank, Washington D.C.

Sarker, Md. Ruhul Amin. 2006. "Rural Financing and Agricultural Credit in Bangladesh: Future Development Strategies for Formal Sector Banks." Dhaka, Bangladesh: University Press Limited.

SEDF (South Asia Enterprise Development Facility). 2006. "Banking Survey of the SME Market in Bangladesh." Dhaka, Bangladesh.

Swiss Re. 2006. "World Insurance in 2005: Moderate Premium Growth, Attractive Profitability." SIGMA Report 5/2006. Swiss Re Economic Research and Consulting, Zurich, Switzerland.

Tamagaki, Kenichi. 2006. "Effectiveness of ITCs on the Dual Objectives of Microfinance." Presented at the International Conference on ICT and Higher Education–E-governance, Japan. [http://www.iac-japan.org/06spring/tamagakip.pdf].

Women's World Banking. 2004. "Remittances: ICICI Builds Technology Based Financial Literacy and Remittance Products for Rural Markets." Innovation Brief. Global Network for Banking Innovation in Microfinance, New York.

World Bank. 1996. "Bangladesh Rural Finance." Report 15484-BD. Washington, D.C.

———. 2002. "Enterprise Survey Database: Bangladesh." Washington, DC.

———. 2003. "Enterprise Survey Database: Rural Bangladesh." Washington, DC.

———. 2004. "Promoting the Rural Non-Farm Sector in Bangladesh." Report 29719-BD. Washington, D.C.

———. 2006a. "Getting Finance in South Asia: An Analysis of the Commercial Banking Sector." South Asia Region, Finance and Private Sector Development Unit, Washington, D.C.

———. 2006b. "Meeting Development Challenges: Renewed Approaches to Rural Finance." Washington, D.C.

———. Financial Sector Development Indicators database. Washington, D.C. [http://www. fsdi.org/].

———. World Development Indicators database. [http://devdata.worldbank.org/dataonline].

World Bank and Bangladesh Enterprise Institute. 2003. "Improving the Investment Climate in Bangladesh." World Bank, Washington, D.C.

Zeitinger, C. P. 2005. "Incentive Systems for Employees of ProCredit Banks." *ProCredit Holding News* (August): 6–7.

Index

ECO-AUDIT
Environmental Benefits Statement

The World Bank is committed to preserving endangered forests and natural resources. The Office of the Publisher has chosen to print *Increasing Access to Rural Finance in Bangladesh* on recycled paper with 30 percent postconsumer fiber in accordance with the recommended standards for paper usage set by the Green Press Initiative, a nonprofit program supporting publishers in using fiber that is not sourced from endangered forests. For more information, visit www.green-pressinitiative.org.

Saved:
- 3 trees
- 2 million BTUs of total energy
- 306 lbs. of CO_2 equivalent
- 1,269 gallons wastewater
- 163 lbs. of solid waste